Monteriggioni
and its territory

Realization: Protagon Editori Toscani
Text: Paolo De Simonis e Gianfranco Molteni
Layout: Pagina
Photos: Fabio Lensini
Drawings: Duccio Santini
Alternative routes graphs: Andrea Rauch
Colour: FIM FotoIncisione Moderna
Print: ALSABA

The authors and the publisher would like to thank
Pietro Clemente, Annamaria Guiducci and Augusto Mazzini
for their contributions (Augusto Mazzini made the drawings
in his text).

ISBN: 88-8024-051-x

Pubblicazione realizzata con il contributo della Banca Monte dei Paschi di Siena

Paolo De Simonis
Gianfranco Molteni

Monteriggioni
and its territory

Protagon Editori Toscani
Siena

To Anna and Annamaria

Creating the grounds for a search for our common identity is a fundamental project on which the City Council of Monteriggioni focused its efforts thus emphasizing the features of this territory.
In several occasions this territory was defined as a land with "thousands of faces", divided in thousands of fragments.
Such considerations often match the real state of this territory, nevertheless these "thousands of faces" can be seen as positive features too, even as reference points, tiles of an outstanding mosaic. A mosaic that presents all the elements and prerequisites to provide to its dwellers and tourists an extraordinarily high level of comfort and life quality in association with a rare balance between landscape, services, economic realities, monuments and occasions to have fun.

Due to objective difficulties even a large part of the inhabitants of this territory does not realize how many potentialities this land has.
On this basis we decided to start some initiatives to promote our territory and among them there is this guide.
Is with great satisfaction that we introduce this work to the reader.
A book which tries to underline not only the well-known landscape and artistic features of Monteriggioni's territory, but to look beyond.
Our wish is that this book will reach our aims. It will, however, show you a land and a community with very different shapes and very dynamic too. A land and a community really worth knowing and in which we love to live and believe.

Paolo Casprini
Mayor of Monteriggioni

The territory of Monteriggioni lays on one of the richer (in historic heritage, art and ambient) areas of the Province of Siena. Among its features, lacking a big urban centre, we can find several villages and hamlets that developed their own personality and carachteristics.
This circumstance, representing an objective administrative complication, is on the other hand a real social and cultural richness. We can imagine many of this territory's villages (Abbadia a Isola, Strove, Santa Colomba, Colleciupi, Poggiolo, Lornano, Scorgiano, just to quote some) as unique "treasure chests" containing incredible jewels of art, tradition and history. 
I found useful to promote such a rich and unknown area to the largest number of people. In this aim this guide was born, in the search for an instrument both scientific and simple. It contains detailed itineraries and descriptions willing to introduce the traveller to an in-depht look to this area.
In this occasion we even designed a particular system of streetsigns to indicate the more interesting places and paths.
Moreover i would like to underline the role that the City Council of Monteriggioni played in the fulfillment of this task. Due to its institutional role the City Council only could provide an equal attention and opportunity to each of its centres.

Donatella Capresi
City Councillor for Culture and Tourism
of Monteriggioni

Luogo della mescolanzà, luogo della vicinanza

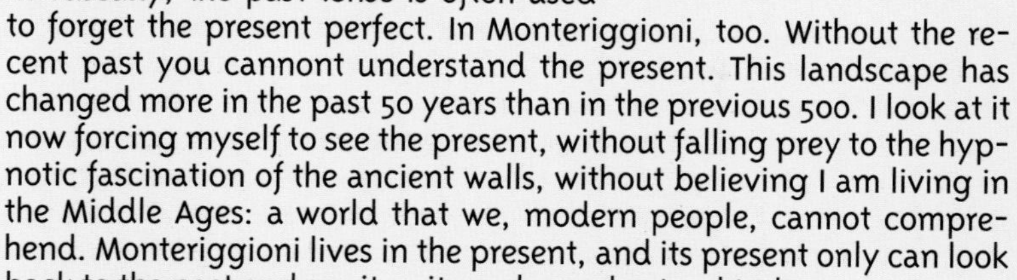

1. *Luogo della mescolanza*

Let us make an effort to see the present. In Tuscany, the past tense is often used to forget the present perfect. In Monteriggioni, too. Without the recent past you cannont understand the present. This landscape has changed more in the past 50 years than in the previous 500. I look at it now forcing myself to see the present, without falling prey to the hypnotic fascination of the ancient walls, without believing I am living in the Middle Ages: a world that we, modern people, cannot comprehend. Monteriggioni lives in the present, and its present only can look back to the past and see it as it can be understood today.
The deepest wound thrust by modern times to this land is the disappearing of the sharecroppers. The countryside is not any longer as Federigo Tozzi described it: animated by those lives scattered among the *poderi*, the carts towed by the huge oxes, people walking ceaselessly, the incessant activity and the utmost care with which fields and woods were tended to. It is upsetting to think about this recent past. The tourist walking past, or even myself, tend to see this landscape as unspoilt, ancient. But what is left of the ancient landscape? The human landscape is not the same. The countryside once hiving with life is now a wilderness. Houses are scattered and far between.
An Englishman is restoring a *casa colonica* down there; two German women live in the next one, another one has fallen to pieces: these are the stories any inhabitant of the place could tell. The tractor proudly works the land, many still live in their *podere*, going to work by car, while the father or grandfather grow vegetables and maybe ducks. The land as a main resource is far, but the countryside is still close: as close as the orchards, the farm animals, the sheep - one could bet the latter come from Sardinia -, the memories of the generations who, only 30-35 years ago, led a different life in a different era: the era of the peasants. The story of the transition has not been properly told yet, the most effective tale is still that by Benigni in *Berlinguer ti voglio bene.* The young find it difficult to imagine: years ago, an exhibition was held in Strove, showing the images of this genealogical history. An exemplary commitment to memory. I was asked to give a speech about it and I prepared a critical attack to nostalgia. More often than not, when communities look at the past they tend to create a legend, by which all that has a spiritual value is in the past, while the present is for matter: one would end up torn in two.
I started with *Le Ricordanze* by Leopardi:

> "[...]Qui non è cosa
> Ch'io vegga o senta, onde un'immagin dentro
> Non torni, e un dolce rimembrar non sorga.
> Dolce per se; ma con dolor sottentra
> Il pensier del presente, un van desio
> Del passato, ancor tristo, e il dire : io fui."

Wishing the past in vain, and not without pain: the paradox of the

peasant world which moulded these lands stands in the superiority of that balance between production and landscape, and in the dramatic social condition its protagonists were forced to live. Tuscany still lives on the heritage of that balance, but agriculture is not the main resource any longer. It is still useful to ask ourselves questions about a balance that created social fractures, but hardly anyone does it these days. The meeting at Strove was successful: after having done my best to convince the audience that one should have a realistic attitude towards the past, I, too, was given a lesson. "Coming from Siena by car, I said, I kept thinking about how long it would taken to cover the same distance on foot, to go to the market for instance. I calculated that it must have taken five hours against today's fifteen minutes." "You might be wrong, professor - someone said - it used to take two hours or even less, we knew a thousand shortcuts without having to follow the route of the motorway." This is the way we should think about that recent past, with no motorway, on foot, without engines running on it and with the sound of oxes, mothers calling out to their children, men shouting to one another in the fields. The pine trees we can see in the woods seem familiar to us, belonging to an ancient landscape: the presence, instead, is the proof that the wood is not looked after nor made good use of any longer. The growth of pine trees has escaped control, and their number is well beyond the original intention of the sharecropper. The trees, too, can be a sign of abandon, and the sardinian shepherds are a sign of a different population: they took over the pastures the sharecroppers had abandoned, and they took their place in the production of the Tuscan *pecorino*. All of this seems plain to see. Nevertheless, while touring around the countryside, the hamlets, the scattered houses, the magic of their conformation is mesmerizing: one needs the infrared glasses of reason, of one's historical memory in order to see all this the way it really is. In spite of everything, still, of course, extraordinarily beautiful. This is how I try to read the landscape I visit, cruising through it by car, as in an experimental account of modern literature, the Joyce way:
sienese suburb traffic lights, here-monteriggioni-begins-without-your-realizing-it. the motorway is monteriggioni. it begins with a *anas* house full of exhaust fumes and a famous graffiti PAOLA I LOVE YOU. monteriggion is a road sign, if you come from the motorway, and a crossroad again with a post office and a modern town hall, roads meeting, place of transit, takes the sienese to florence and the florentines to siena, but also unwinds itself towards the montagnola, land of passage for the reapers in maremma today tanned bathers, nostalgia of the middle ages when armed enemies would cross these lands killing peasants, stealing goods and raping women, a ring road where the exhaust fumes rise high up to the skies, it's monteriggioni. coop, conad, via togliatti industrial and commercial area, in the still rural hamlets and ancient phone boxes, adverts, signs, we cannot go wrong about what era we are in. the *rovi* (blackberries) are called *roghi* here, a sign of the abandon, a landscape not tended to, they invade the ditches and the side of the road. carlo poni used to say that *fossi e cavedagne benedicon le campagne*, countryside of non-existing world but lippi would also say, there's no blessing. railway castellina scalo, trasqua swimming pool, etrusco night club, scene of ad-

venturous nights and *casello anas*, this is also monteriggioni today, fago furs, chianti of the sienese hills, banca toscana, etruscan tombs signposted, at badia isola romanesque jewel you can get a discount on oil at the petrol station. in the heel of this island of romanesque building overlooking the open fields a tractor separates us from the past, five cars parked by the church a suzuki, a simca, a seat, an opel, an alfa romeo, near by a well tended vegetable garden with pigeons, and right behind, amidst the silence of the romanesque walls close in space but far away in time there is a wonderful fig tree emanating a wonderful scent. clothes on a line huge iron structures bring electricity, at scorgiano there is the *astronave* (a restaurant), the only adequate name for what this land is today. silos, nisi agricoltura, stop at 150 metes, hunting allowed, abandoned schools, a varied landscape, cypress trees never abandoning us. high hills overlook lower hills, colle in the distance the profile of poggibonsi, on the other side the montagnola, higher up. amongst cities and mountains and soft hills monteriggioni stands, the name of a muche larger territory, mixing many sides of tuscany, towers and castles, vineyards and olive groves, seep and wheat, coop and *chiantideicollisenesi*, rural banks and small and large estates. monteriggioni a land of production and trade, *blended* as a land must be when it contains belverde and the poggiolo, the station of castellina and santa colomba, the *superstrada* and te track with the cypress trees announcing Lornano for those who come from the *Chiantigiana* road, land of the romanesque and of the villa at Basciano, land of Lornano and Badesse, land of Uopini also known as 'Opini' - a suburb where I saw my first *bruscello* twenty years ago - 'opini' a small world celebrating the beginning of a different type of personal service, everywhere a different celebration and everywhere the same festivity as people enjoy good food; celebrating liberation from poverty; one municipal community with a hundred villagers and each village individually celebrating together its sense of unity; in good times and bad, at times resigned to circumstances and at times remembering the past, a place liberated and governed by communists who celebrate their sense of unity. In this its present state, with its unpleasant exhaust fumes and odours, discarded plastic bottles near the forests, areas of undergrowth and wild unkept pine woods, where Sardinian sheep roam, amid discarded television sets, cypresses and strangers; a place seemingly mediaeval, inhabited by the sons of earthy farmers, where municipal refuse disposal containers and lines of vines, unlike those of the past, now sit side by side. Nothwithstanding all this, they still make good wine, and despite all Monteriggioni knows how to retain it antique heritage. They continue to live to day as in the 1200's even with a Swatch watch on the wrist.
The same happens in Castiglione Ghinibaldi and many other castellated towns with bell gables and towers, in this well populated area where people live and co-existing in small communities. This quotation of Federigo Tozzi comes to mind:
"They lived in a house constructed inside an ancient tower constructed of rocks. The farmyard was located adjacent to the tower. A pig with rosy skin and sparsely covered with shiny hairs, grovelling in the muck and grunting continuously in a state of complete happiness. Four skinny fowls peck at goodness knows what, under a pear tree

with white blossom. We could smell the unpleasant odour of the walled town. Renzo was hoeing. Maria was in her room weaving" (from *Cose e persone, Adele*). Weaving seems to be something of the past. Maria in this day and age is in the television room.

2. *Luogo della vicinanza*
This is certainly not what I am accustomed to see when I look at Monteriggioni. I only see it as I have described it because I am observant. I am aware of the changes especially, in the attitudes of the communities who, when they describe things invent rather than relate and speak without thinking or considering what they are saying. What does Monteriggioni mean to me? I, who have become a citizen of Siena, who came from the country like the sheep from Cagliari, which Fernand Braudel defined as 'a window looking at the Mediterranean'. As I travel in my motor car on the highway to Florence, Torino or wherever, I can see Monteriggioni the old walled and turreted city, a sentinel, a commanding presence in the neighbourhood. This neighbourliness has become a matter of affection because of my familiarity with what lies behind the walls; a small village which fights to retain its character; the gates of the town offer framed views of the surrounding countryside. Even the Divine Comedy refers to, these views which fire the imagination; the pleasures of walking around the town walls, among the friendly undergrowth and olive trees; passing by the stones of the wall which have for centuries watched over the passage of time and which have been renewed here and there by our contemporaries keen to retain their traditional qualities. When we speak of these spaces, we measure them in terms of something neutral or something geometric. There is, as the French anthropologist Marc Augè writes, a *non place* of excessive modernity, and also places which have quality and spaces for daily life. There are places which stimulate feelings of affection where distance is irrelevant, whether they are cold or hot, near or far. We could make something special of these delightful places which give us so much pleasure when we are near them. When I taught at the teachers College of Iglesias, each day I had to travel nearly 70 km . to get there and 70 km. to return to my home in Cagliari. I made the journey with my colleges, as one does everywhere, and we each had our own special landmarks which were as it were signs of recognition and indicative of the approaching destination. These were especially recognisable during the return trip.
At Siena, on the southern section of the highway we had chosen a place we liked in an area of special interest, on a hill with particularly clayey soil, similar to that of the Crete, and on which there was a solitary tree. The spot was easy to find and often frequented by parents needing to stop briefly to rest and console their young children who might need relaxation while on a long journey. Among our friends that place on the hill became, and is still known as "Cirese's Tree". Alberto Cirese, who in the years 72 -74 was professor of Cultural Anthropology at the Faculty of Letters at Siena, and who often visited the city when travelling to the area from Rome, considered that tree and that hill a sign of his return, a sign of his arrival at a place he was anxious and waiting to see. Our children also used the same name as if to remind us of our student days. Goodness knows how many others have

used the same place, the hill and that tree to stimulate and remind one of the past. Anyway that tree has now disappeared and probably someone or some traveller still feels a sense of loneliness because the hill has lost its ability to signal an emotion. As if to repair this sense of loss a new tree has now taken its place, a tree which however seems to need assistance to keep alive. Even this new arrival is in the process of becoming a legend, although it is in the midst of exhaust fumes, asphalt, and is a 'no place'. Its presence in that spot is considered by the famous anthropologist Ernest De Martino as something domestic, something for which he says we feel a need, something which makes us feel at home, something personal which the outside hard and closed world can never take from us. The turreted castle with its rounded walls, outstanding and prominent during the day and even during part of the night, has always marked an important position to the north. It is a place that does not disappear with time and in this area it is in fact a place of special beauty. Monteriggioni for me is the tower that beckons the attention of passing visitors because of its imposing position. I once suggested that one should look at the contrasts around us as if looking into a mirror, because looking has become a form of banality and wonder has become commonplace. Can we imagine the *presence* which the enclosing walls offers us as we approach the year 2000. What passes through our minds as we turn to look while travelling along the Cassia; thoughts which are so strong that they induce the *syndrome of Stendhal,* do we feel the loss of control as if in a vortex, a meeting of time and space like in a gyro which hold both simultaneously. Arriving at Siena, my new home, which is only several hundred metres from the boundary of the comune of Monteriggioni and so close that it almost forms a part of Siena, we have made it our business to show our children, even from early childhood, those imposing surrounding walls, saying " look at the fortress of Monteriggioni, look we have almost arrived we are nearly home".
In fact I still continue to say the same thing, even if quietly to myself, whenever I return alone to Siena by car. Probably even my children, now grownup also repeat the same phrase. Maybe even teachers travelling the same route think the same thoughts as they pass Colle and Poggibonsi. This castle town stimulates the pleasant prospect of home-coming, and distracts boredom. We call the town a castle although in fact it is not a true castle, but because it has the effect of a fairy tale, a place of importance in ones memory and because it awakens the imagination. It is really to this place, with its elevated position in the ever changing landscape, both unimportant and prominent, always indifferent and beautiful, which inevitably attracts attention. It is this place which has inherited the function by virtue of its location of comforting passing Sienese and which although different makes them feel almost at home and gives them a sense of arrival.
Certainly this castle town gives great pleasure especially to children who seeing it feel a sense of home coming. It is like the castle of the prince and princess
whose bedtime stories are read to them at night to reassure a peaceful night's sleep.

Pietro Clemente

The Lions of Basciano

To stay off the beaten track often has a different meaning from the old saying: in the case of aterritory, it almost always means to discover (or re-discover) not the places themselves, but the way to get near them and establish a relationship between them and their historical and physical environment. The stops on the way are important, not the final destination. If one is not driving, and is morevoer accompanied by two friends whise culture is fertile and whose eye is inquisitive, one's attention is constantly stimulated: everything is worth looking at again, the way we do on a journey through an unknown territory. When everything is interesting: the castle and the pavement, the profiles of the hills and an undecipherable sign. If the place is near home one re-discovers how useful it is to forget, if it gives one the joy of seeing again for the first time. That is how that day, a sunday morning dedicated to a morsel of Monteriggioni, it was decided (or maybe it was done without making a decision) to cut a section of that bizarre territory, with many centres but without one centre: " a diffuse settlement, frequent but dispersed, without a concentration of large villages, without open spaces in the countryside, with a recurring promiscuity of woods and fields" are the words that Paolo Cammarosano used to describe it in a memorable essay. To avoid the closed circle of the walls of Monteriggioni, belly-button of an invisible body, but inevitable center around which everything goes: as it happens around a vacuum, a crater, a small, innocuous maelstrom; and to avoid the main roads - the Cassia and, above all, the *superstrada* - to take the unbeaten track. So, from the Chiantigiana, at Poggiarello, down to the left towards Basciano. On the way is the Villa Sansedoni at Basciano; to get to it, we do not enter the main gate, we take a side road instead, and we stop just under the front garden, which needs tending to: the vegetation is scruffy, the terracotta vases are crippled. The chapel shares the misery of the servant's quarters. On the other hand, the façade looks restored: maybe so are the interiors, which is closed and unverifiable. We can guess a probably "social" use, maybe "cultural": it belongs to the *Amministrazione provinciale.* Turning round, we find ourselves in the back garden, even scruffier than the front, with an invasive little wood. The little gates between the two sides are flanked by two brick pilasters with two stone lions on top, much older than the villa itself, which was built in the mid eighteenth century. They are in fact gargoyles in upright position.

The posture makes the lions seem ridiculous, inspite of their mysterious origin: uselessly rampants, with that truncated pyramid attached to their bottom, which once upon a time used to make them jut out of some wall.

We set off again, slightly bewildered (at least, I am) thinking that that was the place from which the erudite Cavalier Ettore Romagnoli, a sansedoni's guest, used to set off on his trips - much more analytical than ours - coming back with painstaking and at times deceitful drawings of villas, castles and churches. At the bottom, the road meets the Staggia river, the Ottarchi bridge of the Siena - Empoli line, which, legend has it, was maybe planned by Stephenson, and the *superstrada*. As soon as we disentangle ourselves from that crossroads, the landscape changes: we have reached the industrial area of the Badesse, the countryside is already behind us. The factories, the warehouses are acceptably scattered around, especially in the most recent part near the *Conad*. In the Sixties and Seventies the territory of Monteriggioni absorbed this kind of productive settlements for which Siena had no room: it was a safety device, like an airbag, for the city. The disaster would have had much bigger proportions if a handful of unarmed opposers (two or three) had not saved Pian del Lago from the indecent proposal of an adventurous industrial ghost town. Today, that precious area would have been ruined and made useless by a few fragments of what some, considering themselves as the noble fathers of the most leftist left wing, prefigured as a "factory employing at least a thousand workers". Thank you, Monteriggioni!

Just along the road, one can go under the railway station and the superstrada and climb up into the real countryside again, as far as Lornano, from which the sighting of the crown of Monteriggioni induces the eye to feel like a voracious camera.

Still ignoring Monteriggioni - time is running out and hunger comes earlier on a sunday - we arrive without distractions (although we can sight the irresistible profile of Castiglion Ghinibaldi) at Abbadia a Isola, under the densely wooded profile of the Monte Maggio. But Abbadia a Isola is too well known. Just two or three roaming thoughts while the eye bulds up the features of the monastery in the block around the church, noticing the ancient coexistence of walls and open spaces, of noble and rural, of works of art and hen-dens: will the Sano di Pietro altarpiece and the *Maestà* by the great (and unknown) Master, now at Colle, be brought back here? Will the latter return "on the right handside on entering the church of Badia all'Isola?" the limpid and professional observations by Alessandro Conti about the halo come back to mind. And, on the threshold of the year 2000 (and not of the stupid "third millennium"), it is impressive to remember the origin of the Abbadia: February the fourth, 1001. Moreover: will the small petrol station along the road survive, as we hope, giving a sense of reality to the place? Off we go, beyond a converted castle near Strove, going down the Elsa valley, where the world of Colle begins: just to turn to the left, towards the back of the Montagnola. The person driving knows there is a church there, I do not. We can see a crane, they are restoring: or converting? It is the romanesque Pieve a Castello. Entry forbidden. The back is better: in the complexity of the building two apses with alternated arches, pillars and an internal loggia can still be identified. Will it be a heavy restoration? There is no sign giving an account of the works undertaken. The sight from the back is magnificent: a long, continuous slope climbs up to a house on top, almost a sky slope without the snow. If they will do a clean job, it will be a nice place to live.

It is time to go back.
I manage to convinve the cultivated and prensile friends to detour to Castiglion Ghinibaldi, although it already difficult to guess the way there.
Once taken the winding road, we get to the building just at the right point: from behind the large curved wall that joins the sqaure block, almost totally closed and without the roof gutter. Did Alvar Aalto see it before his "Kulttuuritalo" (Culture Home, Helsinki 1955-58) during one of his many journeys around Tuscany? For sure, his search for the "cultivated primitivism" could not have found anything more

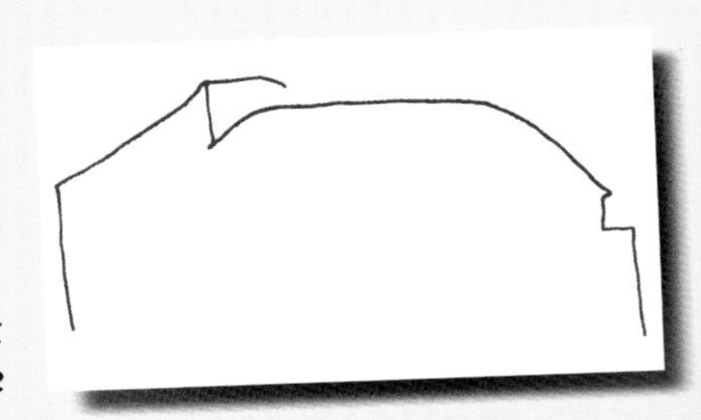

poignant. Almost the same curve, the same profile: most of all, the same compressed and expressive sense of space, the same dryness, elegant and strong at the same time.
Turning the corner, we pass through the XVI century portal into the yard with the double porch, also elegant and dry, luckily imperfect and lived. I do not want to create commotion, but it does remind me the "absolute imperfect" coined by Manfredo Tafuri for Francesco di Giorgio. A building created on/with another one, almost an evident and paradoxical upturning: as if the curved duegentesque block had joined the squarer cinquecentesque block. From the porches, where the life of those still inhabiting them has accumulated an almost theatrical arrangement of tables and chaires, kitchen furniture, iron and plastic armchairs, flower vases and sewing machine without it offending the eye, we take the steps to the top.
Maybe it is a fixation, but it reminds me of Cuna.
There is the trace of more archaic antecedents. The coats of arms recall the history of the place: the Tolomei coat of arms talks of two of the daughters of Ghinnibaldo and Sapia (*Divina Commedia*, Purgatory, XIII) who were both married to members of the Tolomei family. And Ghinibaldo who in 1265 "to redeem his sins", and those of his wife and daughters Diambra, Raniera, Baldesca, Margherita and Andrea, founded a hospital in the castle, so near the Via Francigena.
We head back to Siena, no more welcomed by the dignified residential outskirts, but filtered through commercial settlements (a sort of Siena-freightyard), even late at the time of its building, compared to other examples in Tuscany, banal and out of their place like the lions of Basciano.

Augusto Mazzini

Florence

Grosseto
Siena
DUCCIO SANTINI

How to read

The Guide opens with some notes by Pietro Clemente and Augusto Mazzini. They travel over Monteriggioni roads again, over their memories and run through what the landscape displays (like the lions of Basciano) or hides (the sharecroppers).

We want to propose a more in-depht look on the territory. We would like to 'force' the tourist to see beyond the 'postcard' views, from the hills of Basciano to the more imposing Monte Maggio, what this land offers.

This book's aim is to 'push' the tourist out of the commonplace, out of the clichés into a more complex frame. This book will reach its purpose when it will seem incomplete to the reader's eyes, when it will no longer answer to all the questions. At that point the tourist will maybe grow into a traveller, crossing the territory in the attempt to dismantle what looks intact and to reconstruct what looks broken.

In the first half of the book ve will find three itineraries: *Anno Domini M.CC.XIII* which analyzes the middle-age heritage of the Monteriggioni castle. Aimed to explain what's behind the high curtain of walls we see from the Siena-Florence freeway (and described by Dante in his *Inferno*). But Monteriggioni's land is not only middle-age and the route (passing through Badesse, Uopini and Quercegrossa) displays the variety of monuments and landscapes. ***Monks, artists and sharecroppers*** pushes as far as the north-western sector of this land (in the *Valdelsa*) in the attempt to bind the ancient abbey of Abbadia a Isola to the recent past and present, to the artisans of Strove, the farmers of Scorgiano, the tradesmen of Castellina Scalo. At last *The ring of the Lake* examines the hamlets (among which Colle Ciupi, Fungaia, Santa Colomba) built around a no longer existant lake, which land was reclaimed in the eighteenth century.

Each route can be covered in a full day using a car. Knowing that, in recent times, different ways of travelling are claiming their own space, we provided a chapter dedicated to the *Alternative routes* that can be followed by foot, horseback, bike or even flown by montgolfier.

In the itineraries' text frequently occurs some reference to geology, animal and vegetal life and to this land's history, we will deal with these themes in the final chapters, *Appendix*.

To ease the reading we used a graphical symbology which is useful to know:

Photos depicting churches and villas are surrounded by a **violet** frame

Photos depicting castles and urban buildings are surrounded by a **green** frame

Photos depicting documents are surrounded by an **orange** frame

 **100**

A page number aside to a sand-glass points to another page probing the argument

 **100**

A page number aside to an arrow signals a detour in the itinerary that can be skipped going to that page.

We also included some descriptions made by famous travellers

E. Romagnoli: engravings of churches and villas

"Seating on a flat relief of a hill facing north-east of the Florentine royal post road [the Cassia of today] passing under it, while the torrent Staggia runs on its back, on the north side...

E. Repetti: descriptions of hamlets

Anno domini M.CC.XIII

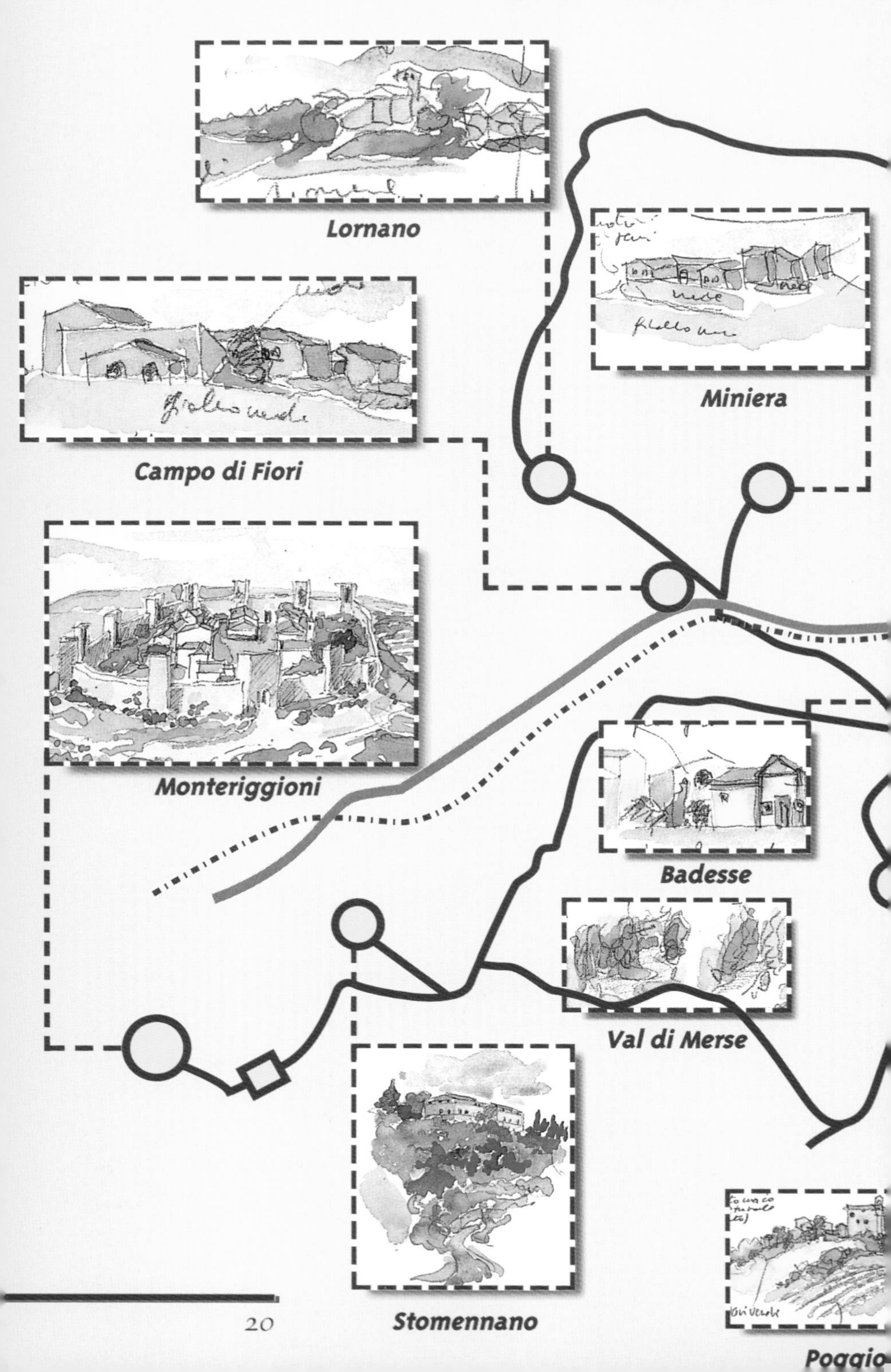

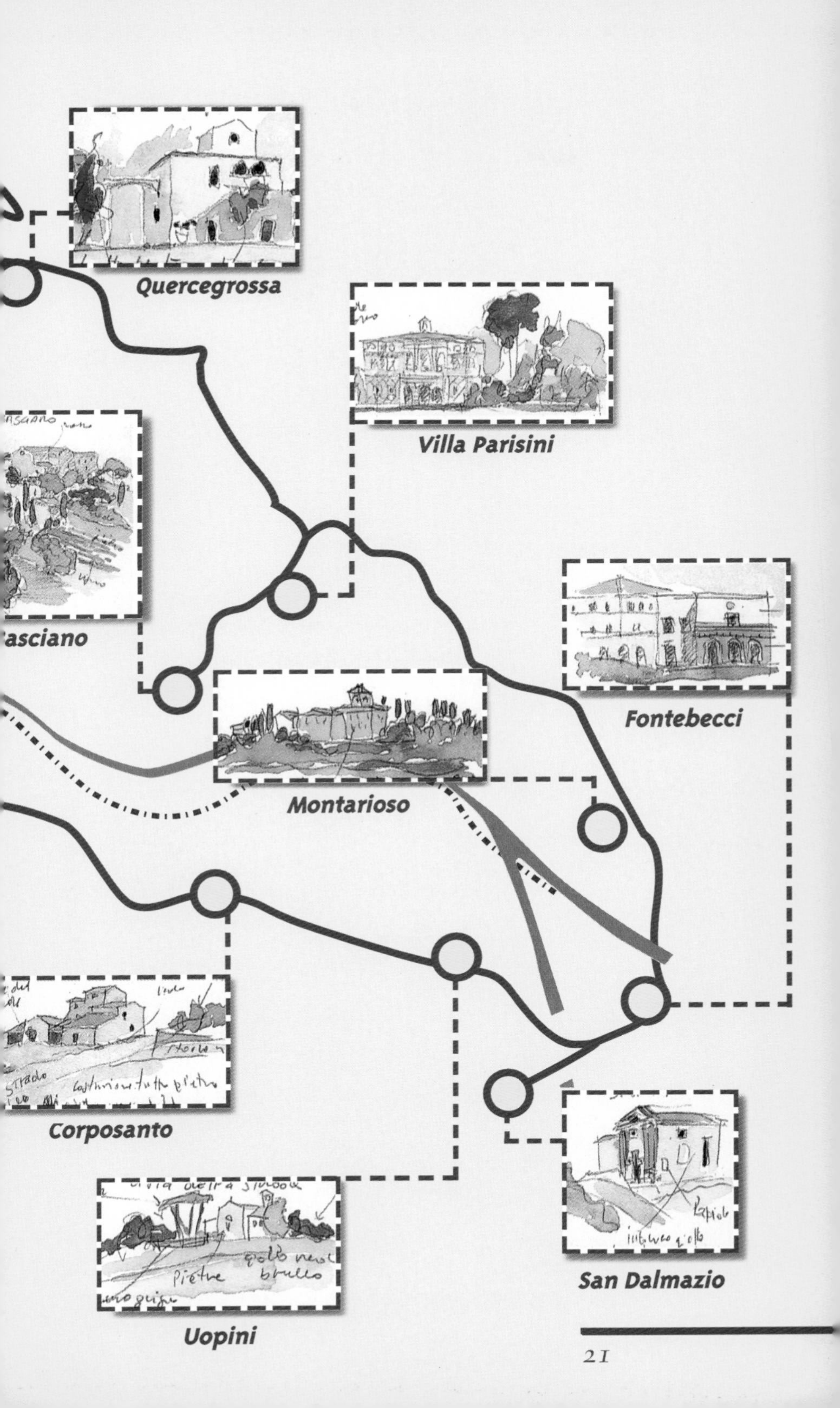
Quercegrossa
Villa Parisini
asciano
Fontebecci
Montarioso
Corposanto
San Dalmazio
Uopini

The visit and the history of the Monteriggioni castle start with this stone, enclosed on the upper left hand side of the gate called "Franca" or "Romea", opening in the south-east side of the town wall. A bigger and far more recent stone is placed on the right of the gate: it commemorates the results of the plebiscite by which, on March 15, 1860, also the people of Monteriggioni voted for the annexion to the State of Piemonte and the Unitary Italian State.

Anno Domini M.cc.xiii, indictione secunda mense martii, existente domino Guelfo Hormanni Paganelli de Porcara Senensium potestate, domino Arnoldo Pisano judice discreto et Ildebrandino Usimbardi camerario Senensium, hoc castrum Montis Regionis in Dei fuit nomine inceptum, et undique postea muro vallatum, propriis Senensis populi laboribus et expensis, per virorum nobilium Ranuccii Crescentii et Orlandi Filippi et Forensis Martini studium et operam diligentem.

"In the month of March of the year of our Lord 1213, in the time of Sir Guelfo di Ermanno di Paganello Porcari Lord Mayor of Siena, of Sir Arlotto from Pisa, wise judge, and of Ildebrando di Usimbardo *camerario* of Siena, this castle of Monteriggioni in the name of our Lord was started and then wholly enclosed by walls. The cost and the works were supported by the people of Siena, under the skilful supervision of the nobles Ranuccio di Crescenzio and Orlando di Filippo and Forese di Martino".

Two commemorating stones, then, distant in time but near in meaning, as both express a will to belong to the state. The first is obviously more specific, as it emphasizes the role of the Siena *comune* in the foundation of the castle. This event was in this way made more solemn because the building *ex novo* of a fortified wall departed from the political and military Sienese custom to adapt already existing structures - as they did in the neighbouring castle of Quercegrossa. The Sienese character of the undertaking was not put at risk by the fact that Guelfo di Ermanno di Paganello was from Pisa: in the Middle Ages the Lord Mayor (*podestà*) appointed for one year only, was a noble man who *must not* belong to local aristocracy, in order to able to run the town holding aloof from the rivalries that were tearing it. Guelfo came from an important aristocratic family of Pisa, from the omonymous hamlet of Porcari; and so did judge Arlotto, whose legal capacity supported the military competence of the *podestà*. The other noblemen mentioned above, Ranuccio di Crescenzio, Orlando di Filippo, Forese di Marino and Ildibrando di Usimbardo, were however Sienese, the latter *camerario*, that is to say at the head of the *Biccherna*, the most important administrative and financial body of the *Comune*.
The date needs an historical interpretation: the year 1213 for

The Romea gate occupies the base of a tower showing, inside the wall, two large arches one on top of the other, as thick as the tower itself. An iron gate could be dropped to stop sudden enemy's attacks. It is also notable the machicolation, slightly decentred, which dropped both solid and liquid projectiles on the assailants.

the founders of Monteriggioni corresponds to 1214 for us. In Siena, Florence and many other towns the beginning of the new year was not on January 1st but on March 25th, the day of Christ's incarnation. Even though the stone does not indicate the day of the month when the castle was founded, historians are able to fix the date between 18th and 24th March, so the date of birth of Monteriggioni castle is for us 1214. The physical placing of the stone could not obviously occur on the castle foundation day but when the building of the defensive walls was well under way.

We now walk inside the castle along the first part of its main axis - via Primo maggio - leading into Piazza Roma, of a rectangular shape, with a *cisterna* (a well) in the middle.

On the right, after the old churchyard, is the church of Santa Maria Assunta, which was built after the castle and which took the name of the old parish church (VII century), once located on the farm land named "Il Santo" (the saint). The building of the new church was however completed in 1235, when the peace terms between Siena and Florence were accepted. At the end of the XIII century it became a *collegiata* church, where several priests lived, and was endowed with some land. After a period of decay, also due to the transit of imperial troops during the war of Siena of 1553, the church was restored between 1597 and 1608 by the parish priest, Franciuoli; other works, among which the restoration of the rectory and the building of the bell tower, were carried out at the end of the XVIII century. The church style shows evidence of the original romanesque style, especially in the external structure. The façade is made of travertine hewn stones, a single-ridged roof with a round window in the centre of the tympanum, made in red bricks with vegetable decorations. The southern side top bears corbels carved as human heads; on that side there are two windows; on the north side there used to be two portals, one which is now closed

179

and visible on the outside. The church is one-naved and ends in a rectangular apse. The ceiling, originally beamed, is now vaulted. A brick arch separates the apse from the rest of the church. The rectory was restored in 1747. The bell tower was erected at the end of the XVIII century by the parish priest Mecacci, who used the stones of the dilapidated church of San Giovanni a Stecchi. The church has undergone such alterations in the course of the centuries that very few are the remains of the ancient

27

times. The present shape has even cancelled any trace of the XVII-XVIII century restorations, including the wall paintings representing Saints by Carlo Amidei (perhaps covered with plaster). The only XV century remains are two marble tabernacles in the shape of temples, walled in by the side of the high altar, on which are engraved the names of the patrons and the dates 1467 and 1477, the first commissioned by the parish priest Ser Simone and the second by Ser Antonio di Domenico. The wooden choir, behind the high altar, shows XVI century architectural elements, in the austere elegance of its classical lines.

After the church, on the right of the entrance of the restaurant il Castello at n. 22, there is a nice portal. Other remarkable portals are on the opposite side, at the numbers 12 and 13. On the short south-east side there are faintly decipherable traces of another church.

"As far as one can see the well preserved in length and heigth *filaretto* of this house - Veltroni Poderetti wrote in 1907 - was the ancient curate church of St John the Evangelist at Stecchi, whose building preceded that of the Castle which was very small, measuring m. 6,60 per m. 3,60. Today it houses a store, the entrance to which is the same as when it was a church, although it was much wider then: traces are visible in the ancient arch, like a cleft in the wall of the existing house, interrupted by a window. The ancient church door was, in style and width, symilar to the one of the existing parish church.
I have heard from the old ones, as Pecci states, that this church had four rooms, two on each side, taking up the whole length of the building. One was the death chamber, the remaining three the sacristy. The four of them were decorated: one by Francesco Vanni, a second one by Rutilio Manetti, and the other two by the pupils of the aforementioned Manetti, but those paintings are all lost today."
In the centre of the square is a cistern: in the well under it there is an iron door which should lead into underground rooms. Like in other historical places, here as well many beliefs have formed themselves about the existence of fascinating spaces and hypogean routes. In the words of Veltroni Poderetti "To the north, where the cemetery is, there is a cave, in which is the entrance to a subterrenean way dug under the Castle itself. [...] Tradition has it that under Monteriggioni there is a roomful of arms."
Oral memory also allows the restoration of the recent past of Monteriggioni, based on the sharecropping system: "There were five peasants, all of them sharecroppers, with their animals and all, who had their farmhouses outside. Large farms. One used to be there [n. 20] and the barn was beside it, where the restaurant is today. In that other restaurant was the *tinaia*, where they used to store the wine. Then, the rest of them where land labourers, working in the farms in the area. Here, where the *enoteca* (wine library) is now, there used to be the blacksmith, a famous one for shoeing the animals. Beside him was the post office [n. 13], and in this large house [n. 15] was the *Carabinieri*'s barracks. All over the square and in the rest of the village it was very different from today, stone-paved everywhere: the ground was gravelled. Here in the square us boys used to meet to play football, on saturdays and sundays. In that other small square [in the second part of Via Primo Maggio, in front of the numbers 19, 21 and 23] the old ones used to say that they used to perform *bruscello*, the *Pia de'Tolomei*, although I have never seen it.

Continuing along the second part of Via Primo Maggio, towards the Florentine Gate, or St John's Gate (Porta Fiorentina o di San Giovanni), we meet on the left a series of medieval buildings, whose origin is made evident by the nice portals and the painstakingly executed *filaretto* at numbers 19, 21 and 23. A small squares opens up just opposite, surrounded by recently restored blocks: better than anywhere else one can identify the area just behind the walls, now occupied by vegetable gardens.
As the street makes a rapid descent, towards the gate we take a turn to the left, into the largo di Fontebranda (where, at n. 5, is the seat of the *Pro Loco* association) introducing to a more intimate section, protected by the stage represented by piazza Roma and via Primo Maggio, extending into via Matteotti. This is where the country roots of the village emerge to the surface: also for the presence of some buildings which do not take the typical shape of village settlements, but represent an unusual transplantation of the farmhouses that we "normally" find in open countryside, such as the structures at n. 5 and n. 7. In front of these last two buildings we resume our dialogue with the Middle Ages: the tower, at n. 2, is an archaic antecedent of a castle. Various stylistic details prove it, such as the lintels of the two windows and the monolytic architrave above the door, with shell-shaped corbels.
Coming back to the Romea gate we conclude the visit of the historical and urbanistic "content" of Monteriggioni, but we set off on a new visit, forcing us to a careful exam of its container: a very pleasant 20 minutes stroll along the external perimeter, following a track in the grass among the olive

trees. A 560 metres walk, rhythmically interrupted by 14 rectangular towers: a fifteenth one is only visible from the inside because it does not jut out, between the second and the third tower, looking from the inside after the oriental gate. We actually walk where the medieval *carbonaie* used to be: a ditch filled with coal (*carbone*), which would be set on fire during attacks when the town was under siege. Documentary evidence proves that this is the site where important pacts were sealed: among these, in July 1221, the anti-Florentine alliance pact between Siena and Poggibonsi.

Only imagination can reconstruct the drawbridge outside the gate: there is documentary evidence of the expenses for the chains, together with other iron devices, in the *Biccherna* books of 1267.
Every year in August, in the occasion of the celebrations for Saint Mary, the representants of the community of Monteriggioni would take their exit from this gate, taking to the Duomo of Siena their offering of candles, like all the rest of the villages: in 1337 Monteriggioni made the generous donation of a 60 pound candle and ten candles of one pound each.
During the 1229-1232 war (uniting Siena, Poggibonsi, Pisa and the emperor Frederick II against Florence, Montepulciano, the Pope, Orvieto and Arezzo) a german mercenary from the imperial army was specifically responsible for the tower and the gate. In the *Biccherna* books, other german soldiers, or coming from Italian regions such as Emilia and Lombardia, are registered as defenders of Monteriggioni. However, as a rule the recruiting only took place in the Sienese territory, and only in the hour of need. The main force were the *pedites*, the infantry, in numbers oscillating between a few dozens and two or three hundreds. The crossbow archers, usually from the Po valley or from Pisa, were much more professionally competent and skilled: their weapons, guarded in felt holders in the palace of the *comune* in Monteriggioni, were provided by the *comune* of Siena. To increase their efficiency, the point of the arrows was covered in tar, set on fire when shot. Magic was also considered an efficient weapon during wartime: "In the summer of 1231 - Cammarosano remembers - a Sienese messenger brought to the army at stance at Monteriggioni a powder, confectioned by certain women, and in the autumn a women from the ally Poggibonsi brewed a *medicine*: certainly, a magic preparation to be spread on the enemy's tents, or the roads they would trod on, or the walls and gates of their castles and towns".

Above all, the itinerary renders noticeable the oval shape of the walls circuit, adapting to the round curves of the hills and following with good approximation a same contour line. The texture of the walls is made of square stones, in rectangular rows, each measuring about 20 x 25 cm: the dimensions are small because of the nature of the stone, travertinous limestone, featuring many internal cavities and therefore presenting uneven resistance. As we proceed towards the top, even lesser are the ashlars of the reconstructed segments.

The structure of the walls consists of two screens with a filling of stones and pebbles in the middle, glued together by mortar, reaching an overall thickness estimated in between one and a half metre and two metres, vertically. To the sides of the towers there is an external interruption of the *filarotti* and an absence of the gripping in the edges: a proof of the fact that they were built after the walls. The square towers are solid up to the peak of the wall curtain, and "shielded", that is to say they do not have the back side. They jut out of the walls, aligning to it on the inside, thus forcing the communication trench to get across them through arched doors. The towers are arranged at short, irregular intervals: 35-40 metres on the east and south-east side and about 80 metres on the north and north-east side. The canonical distance should, in fact, be around 40 and 80 metres: the length corresponding to the range of bows and crossbows manou-

The route corresponds to an upsetting of the usual optical perception of Monteriggioni: that from the long distance, by which the profile of the walls appears both as a part of the landscape and as an abstract archetype of the Middle Ages at war. On the other hand, a closer investigation involves a pragmatic interpretation which, from the panoramic view to a close up, reveals itself with the unmercifulness of the minimal detail, generating a different fascination, a close relative to analysis. The identification of Monteriggioni with the Middle Ages, to tell the truth, is not just a result of an interpretative impressionism or naïf historic projections. These walls are, as a matter of fact, one of the utmost monuments of the medieval architectural culture in Tuscany. And not only for their substantial integrity. Even as they were built, they were considered an extraordinary achievement. This is confirmed by their prestigious, and only, medieval image, generated by the fact that they inspired one of Dante's metaphors. In the famous passage from the XXXI canto of *Inferno*, when, as he is crossing the barrier towards the central ditch, the poet hears in the silence the sound of a horn, more powerful than that of Orlando at Roncisvalle and he thinks he sees "many tall towers". They are instead, Virgil explains, giants, standing "in the well around the slope/ from their belly button downwards all of them".

"Come quando la nebbia si dissipa,
lo sguardo a poco a poco raffigura
ciò che cela il vapor che l'aere stipa,

così forando l'aura grossa e scura,
più e più appressando ver la sponda,
fuggìemi errore e crescìemi paura:

però che come sulla cerchia tonda
Monteriggion di torri si corona,
così 'n la proda che 'l pozzo circonda

torreggiavan di mezza la persona
li orribili giganti, cui minaccia
Giove dal cielo ancora quando tona."

vered by the defenders on the flank coverage, made easier by the projection of the towers.
During the walk, as it were, we find ourselves in the same visual condition as the besiegers: less vulnerable, here on the north side, for the lack of a tower on the corner, and for the convex shape of the walls. On this stretch we can still see, under the present coping, the original battle-

ments. Almost at the end of this sid
between the western door and th
first tower on the left, there is a ta
and narrow opening at the bottor
partially dug in, with ashlars gettir
closer at the top and corbels. W
come to the Florentine gate, or *Por*
di San Giovanni: a simple roun
arch, directly opened in the wal
particularly refined in this point, fo
lowed on the inside by a lowere
arch. On the left of the gate, on wh
appear to be the remains of a wa
there are evident traces of the *rivel.*
no, or of a double gate: on top, v
can still read the battlements, walle
in, and the traces of a *bertesca*. W
continue along the south side, whic
between August 27 and 28 1554, w
badly damaged by Florentine ca
nons. Adjacent to the third tower, a
ter the San Giovanni gate, there
what most probably was the thi
gate to castle: typologically ve
similar to the San Giovanni gat
with a full arch and a slightly ogiv
estradosso. This opening, however,
only entirely visible on the inside. C
our external route only the termin
arch emerges, as the lower part w
dug in the earth accumulated und
the walls between the XV and X
century: a "soft" trick deviced
prevent the defensive enclosure fro
falling on the defenders. The la
sign of such events is visible on th
external right side of the first tow
on the left of the oriental gate: c
top, there is a XVI century brick ori
opening, from where a weapon w
aimed against possible attackers.

Castello (castle): a diminutive of the Latin castrum. Emigrated into Arabic, it became qasr, and finally repatriated in the form cassero.
Merlo (battlement): from the medieval Latin mergula, "merletto della veste (lace trimming). Some forms of this symmetrical interruption in the walls, behind which the defenders would hide, where also called a trina or a pizzo, two other words meaning lace.
Bertesca: first a wooden structure, succesively made of stone, jutting out of the walls in those points needing a stronger defence. It favoured sighting and defence by dropping things.
Piombatoio: a space from which solid and liquid projectiles were dropped (boiling water, oil and tar).
Scarpa: inclined wedge added to the base of the walls to make them stronger, eliminate dead corners in front and prevent mobile towers from getting close.
Rivellino: additional fortification, in the shape of a "V" or rectangular, placed before a gate.

The towers were raised about 10 metres above the enclosure, and the walls themselves were ten metres high, with a square battlement. The building of the compound started in 1214, and it prolonged along the course of the century. To complete its ideal reconstruction, we should take into account the defensive value of various removable wooden structures, such as the *bertesche* and all the so-called "jutting out contrivances". Like for other contemporary, important building enterprises, there was an "Opera of Monteriggioni" directed by an *operarius* or by a committee of *operarii*, in charge for six months or a year at the most. The defensive efficacy of Monteriggioni gained value in the course of the centuries also through the ascertainment of the fact that its conquer was only possible with deceipt: in the reality of 1554, but also in several half-legendary tales. Tradition has it that in 1478 a peasant coming back from collecting wood revealed the identity of a bunch of Florentines who almost managed to gain access exhibiting forged letters: such goal was reached in 1482 by some Sienese political exiles. Four of them pretended to be hunters looking for their lost dog, thus getting the gate opened for them, and starting to call the animal: that was the agreed sign for other fourty comrades hiding in the vicinity.
The following conquer of Monteriggioni knew episodes of brutal violence, related in Allegretto Allegretti's chronicle: "those inside would not surrender; more citizens were siezed, than Fathers, Brothers and Relatives of those inside, to thrust them forward, when those inside battled with blowpipes, slings and crossbows". Thus, they would have been the first to die, but the besieged declared that each ...

of them would kill the other's brother, in order not to stain their hands with their own blood. The walls were lowered between the XV and XVI century, to meet the new requirements of the military art, which now had to take into account the importance of artillery. The utility of the *carbonaie* was therefore much lessened. A description by Concini, written on September 1, 1554, relates of walls towering above a steep slope, 32 *braccia* (about 20 metres) high, and between this and the walls, "a small ditch round it, to receive the arquebuses." After having suffered the consequences of the 1554 siege, the walls progressively deteriorated until they were used as building material: the wall of the graveyard on the north side was built in 1847 with ashlars from the walls. The same thing happened, during at least the course of the entire XIX century, for various buildings inside the castle. Only in this century was the trend inverted: a first restoration to the walls, at the very beginning of the century, and a rise of the towers of 7-8 metres, between the 20s and the 30s.

From Monteriggioni, we go down to the junction with the Cassia road, continuing along it in the direction of Siena. A little further on, on the left, is the wide façade of the villa "La Posta": built from 1828 to 1836, on a project by the Sienese Alessandro Doveri, as a post-stage for horses, its function was soon made obsolete (in the second half of the century) by the opening of the Siena-Empoli railway line. After less than a kilometre, on the left, is the turning to

Stomennano

"This place, previously owned by the Sienese noble family of the Accarigi, and now enriched by beautiful cultivations, statues and grand avenues by the Griccioli of Siena [...] made itself known for the treaty of peace between the Sienese and the Florentine, when the latters were besieging Monteriggioni, stipulated on June 11, 1254 in the church of Stomennano.."

The name of the place appears for the first time in a document of 1059. In the following century, as in 1164 it was passed from the Soarzi family to the bishop and the *comune*

of Siena, it was the centre of a *curtis* (bailey) and, perhaps, also the seat of a castle: a clue to this could be the thick wall now inside the Griccioli villa, representing its last architectural arrangement.

Preceded by a beautiful boulevard lined by century-old cypress trees, the villa is composed of two separated blocks, on a rectangular plan, united by a balustrade supported by two columns with architrave, acting as a theatrical wing between the drive and the garden: the villa to the left, the outbuildings (cellars, warehouses) to the right. Slightly detached is the patrician chapel in Renaissance style: the façade is divided by pilaster strips and the entrance is surmounted by a triangular pediment. The garden in front of the villa alternates terraces and fountains, while the back garden presents the divisions typical of the Italianate garden. After the turning to Stomennano, the scenery around

the Cassia becomes greener and more secluded.

Shortly after the km 237, and as the valley opens up again,

The government of the House of Lorena had established that in the vicinity of the gorge called "di Val di Merse", proverbially of ill repute as a place for assaults and ambushes, a picket of soldiers should have their seat. Still at the beginning of this century, according to Veltroni Poderetti, "in Siena we hear repeated everyday: 'Surely we are not in the Val di Mersa?' and also: 'There are more gentlemen in val di Mersa'". After all, Venerosi Pesciolini recalled how the whole area between Monteriggioni and Badesse was considered as risky: "the water course of the Staggia, deeper and wilder than today, and the dense woods made this place one of the most dangerous on the Francigena route, especially at the Lappeto passage where - as the quote goes in the *statuto dei viari* - *occasione multorum aquarum que ibi congregatur* many would drown, and *occasione nemoris et obscuratione ipsius* many were robbed".

the Cassia forms, with two gravel roads, a crossroads, which is today of negligible importance in road traffic, but which bears historical significance. The road coming from the right is in fact on the route of the old Francigena, identifying itself with the Cassia from here onwards. Our itinerary, however, continues on the road coming from the left, corresponding to a junction with the new Francigena. Surrounded by beautiful landscape we climb up to

Poggiolo

"Seating on a flat a hill facing nort the Florentine ro road [the Cassia c passing under it, torrent Staggia ru back, on the nor This Poggiolo is r a document of M 1302, written in S belonging to the the Santuccio or of the Tralisse in that town. It is a donation made to that monastery of two lot one of which situated in the Staggia plain in a place named Pontevecchio, and the other one in th St Maria del Poggiolo, in a place called Cagio... in 1640 it had 149 inhabitants, who in 183 creased to 253 individuals".

Originally also called Porghiano, it was a castle of the bishops of Siena, to whom it was confirmed by Clemente III in 1189 and by Innocentius III in 1210.

The church, dedicated to St mary, is reported in documents as early as the XIII century. Starting from the year 1300, it is called Santa Maria al Poggiolo. In 1375 it was rebuilt, probably due to the increase in population, and in 1380 its first rector was nominated. Starting from 1564 until 1804, to to make for the scantiness of the revenues, it was united to the parish church of SS Quirico and Giulitta in Siena. In 1879 the falling of the bell tower caused heavy damages to the building, and the death of a few parishioners, as the priest Merlotti hands down to us in his dramatic reconstruction: "it was the Sunday before Lent (February 23), and the most impetuous wind ever to be record-

ed in man's memory in this land, and the water was streaming down from the sky in rivers; many refrained from going to church but of the few who went just two, the priest celebrating the office and another individual lost their lives in the debris. Others were carried half alive in the houses nearby ceased living very soon, as soon as they received the last sacraments of the Church; others were wounded, up to the number of thirtyeight. Those were mostly cured at home by four doctors coming from Siena for that purpose, and others, more seriously injured, were carried to and cured in the Hospital of Siena: and all this at the expense of the meritorious *comune* of Monteriggioni, the lord mayor of which was at the time the industrious and merciful Signor Ernesto Nasimbeni, who in such circumstances surpassed himself, and truthfully deserved every praise for the assis-

tance to his communists (sic!.
and for the solicitudes which
he untiredly bestowed on the
aforementioned injured".
At the end of the same year the
church was consolidated, bu
the works were still being carried out at the time of the
Memorie by Merlotti (1881).
The building has a façade
with the portal surmounted by
a lunette and a round window
in the centre. The one-navec
interior, with a hammerbean
ceiling, still has three altars
the high altar, in stucco, i:
dated 1830; the lateral one:
contain modern images substituting the lost ancient works o
art, the *Sacred Heart* (on the
right) and the *Virgin with Child* (on the left). the righ
altar is from 1675. The paintings preserved today inside
the church, on the inner façade, were not commissionec
for this church, to which they were moved after the
mid-eighteenth century. They are two altarpieces by
Rutilio Manetti of remarkable importance, as they give
evidence of two very different phases in the activity o
the Sienese painter, a sharp-eyed divulger of car
avaggesque naturalism in the provinces. The *Madonn*
with Child and the Saints Ansano, Maddalena, Bernardi
no e Caterina da Siena, is in fact signed and dated 1614
We notice in the painting a sharp attention in describ
ing "things", accompanying the ability to play with
shadows and lights, revealing materials and complex
ions through the chiaroscuro. The view of Siena appear
ing in the background at the centre is particularl
evocative. We recognize, painstakingly outlined, th
Camollia gate, the church of San Domenico and the Duo
mo. The second canvas, also very large and also comin
from a church in town, belongs to a much later period
It represents the *Visions of the blessed Bernard*
Tolomei, the founder of the olivetan benedictines. Th
scene abridges two episodes related to the life of th

blessed bernardo: the apparition of the Crucifix during meditation and the vision, on the upper right hand side, of the ladder by which some olivetan monks ascend to Heavens. The painting is softer, the landscapes have gentler shades and the intensity of the religious feeling accompanies the lucid naturalistic description.

The present road does not continue directly from the small settlment. It is necessary to retrace our steps, descending to the junction where the sign "Poggiolo" is, and turn left here. On a steep gravel road again, we rapidly get to the opposide side until we reach the tarmack of the Strada Provinciale n. 119 "delle Badesse", probably repeating the route of the new Francigena. We continue to the right, in the direction of Siena, at first at the bottom of the valley and then climbing up again along a ridge with ample views. A medieval post-stage of restoration was annexed to the curch of the Sacred Body: unfortunately, this place was sadly known for very different reasons. It was here, in fact, that public executions would take place: exemplarly visible here, thus retaining their efficacy as a deterrent for crooks, whose destiny was to be hanged if they "broke the road", that is to say mugged and robbed travellers.

We continue and meet

Uopini

Local tradition has the toponym coming from a pagan persistence, linked to the place where a temple dedicated to the goddess Opi used to be.
Following a diversion on the left, with a signpost indicating the *campo sportivo*, we reach the church of the saints Marcellino, Pietro and Erasmo, already existing in the XII century. Its historical events, during the middle ages, always seem related to the neighbouring church of San Dalmazio, more prosperous and populated. The precarious conditions of the church made it the object of various patronages from the XVIII century onwards, until in 1860 the church was under royal patronage. Preceded by ample steps, the façade still preserves the original exterior, recuperated under a coat a

plaster in the 40s: large stones of travertine and sandstone. The portal is surmounted by a lunette in which is a recent bas-relief, by Luciana Staderini. On the right side of the church, the figure of a saint saint, inside a hollow indicating an ancient access to the church, is by the same artist.

Pellegrino (Pilgrim): *from the Latin* per *and* agere; *that is to say, "he who goes through the fields", "beyond the urban territory". But also, through a metaphor, "beyond earthly life".*
Palmiere: *a pilgrim to the holy Land, from the palms he would gather in Gerico.*
Romeo: *a pilgrim to Rome, featuring St Peter's keys.*
Jacquot: *a pilgrim to Compostela, featuring St James's shell.*
Bisaccia: *shoulder bag. From the Latin* bis *and* saccus, *meaning double bag.*
Bordone: *the pilgrim's walking stick, through a metaphor from the Latin* burdo, *mule.*
Scarsella: *leather belt bag, to guard money in.*
Strada: *from the Latin (via)* strata, *paved road.*

The geometrical decorations engraved on the stone profiles of the lunette are Romanesque persistences. A surviving historical evidence of the various modifications to the church carried out in the course of the centuries are the door of the polychrome marble tabernacle, once on the high altar, now enclosed in the wall at the end; and the three paintings which used to embellish the altars. These were part of the interventions by the parish priest Cristoforo Bizzarri in 1696 to renovate the internal setting (mentioned in the plaque in the sacristy). The painting representing the *Assumption of the Virgin with the Saints Marcellino, Pietro and Erasmo* is dedicated to the eponymous saints; once on the high altar, it is a work by the Sienese Lorenzo Feliciati, active at the beginning of the XVIII century. The painting is a typical product of the artist, expressing strictly devotional themes in conventional form and with baroque reminiscences in the bright chromatic values. Of inferior quality is the *Crucifixion with the Magdalene and the Saints Bernardino and Catherine adoring the Madonna*, also painted by an XVIII century Sienese artist, who portrays the saints in stiff postures.

At Uopini there was a "spedaletto", a shelter for pilgrims and travellers; documentary evidence of 1440 states that it was equipped with eight beds, a barn and a room for the keeper. In that place, founded by the Blessed Giovanni Colombini, an oratory in his memory was erected at the end of the XVI century: on the right hand side, along the provincial road, almost at the end of the village. An altarpiece depicting the *Virgin in glory with St Bartholomew and the Blessed Giovanni Colombini* was commissioned to Vincenzo Rustici and placed in the oratory at the end of the works, around 1590-91.The painting appears strongly influenced by the style of Alessandro Casolani, Vincenzo's brother-in-law, in the rhythmic distribution of the figures in a pyramidal composition deriving from classical tradition, and in the devotional intonation of the scene, narrated using limpid chromatic tones: in the background, at the centre, an evocative view of the Monte Maggio.

From Uopini we procedd until the Cassia, where we detour on the right to the church of

S. Dalmazio

This is a consistent and complete example of an eighteenth century structure, both in the architecture and in the internal decorations. The parish church is mentioned in a document of 1086, and in 1208 the oath for peace between the Sienese and the Florentines was ratified here. The façade, in Renaissance style, alternates bricks on plaster: the pilaster strips, the triangular tympanum, the three little windows. The interior is pleasanlty homogeneous: sumptuos white stuccos alternate with pictorial decorations. Ten canvases depict the *Stories of the Virgin.* These are, starting from the left wall from the entrance: *The Immaculate Conception, the Circumcision of Jesus as a child, the Flight into Egypt, Saint Ansano and the Virgin, the Assumption of the Virgin, the Nativity of Mary* (the last two on both sides of the high altar), the *Presentation of Mary to the Temple,* the Annunciation, *the Visitation, the Marriage of the Virgin.* The hands of more than one artist, all up-to-date with the latest baroque innovations, are detectable in the cycle, to be placed chronologically between the second half of the XVII century and the beginning of the next century. On the high altar a glory of angels surrounds the *Virgin with child,* a polychrome terracotta bas-relief from the XVI century, the object of popular devotion. Tradition has it that the terracotta was fortuitously found in 1645 in the ruins of an oratory nearby. Ascanio Piccolomini, then the bishop of Siena, wanted the sacred image to be an object of cult. Ten years later, the building of the church started. Above, *God the Father with cherubs* leans out from a broken tympanum. The side altars are simpler, embellished by scrolls. On the inner façade are two modest canvases representing *Saint Catherine of Siena and Saint Bernardino,* the work of a Sienese painter from the XVIII century.

We now get back in the direction of Siena, until the point where the Chiantigiana, coming from the left, meets the Cassia. The intensity of today's traffic confirms the historical role of this important crossroads approaching Siena, but it also hides its main architectural feature: the small, three-arched porch in red bricks, which gave shelter to the water of

Fonte Becci

"It is one of the most ancient public fountains ever built by the Sienese, in 1228, and more than once restored at public expense, in 1309, 1338, 1418 and 1575. Here, on January 20 1313 the Sienese valiantly fought against Henry VII's army; and from here, as early as 1333, the horse race would start for the mid-august Palio."

Medieval sources mention a hostel at Fonte Becci: sometimes called a hotel, other times a tavern, they might refer to the same structure performing more than one function. Owned by the Santa Maria della Scala (the ancient Sienese hospital), the hotel is mentioned as early as the first decades of the XIV century for a row taking place at Santa Petronilla where the landlord of Fontebecci, Blaxio di Dino, was beaten up. It is then often mentioned in rent contracts issued by the Santa Maria della Scala to various innkeepers and landlors. We know that in 1353 the hotel also owns vieyards and some land, to provide produce for its guests. When vineyards and land were not sufficient, the innkeeper did not mind smuggling supplies to avoid paying toll, especially being near the border to Florence, as was the case at Fontebecci. The keeping of the hotel must pay well if Nanni di Biagio, landlord at Fontebecci, could buy in 1412 a "posisione" (a possession) from the hospital itself at San Miniato, for 130 florins. The landlords' gains did not always come from an honest source: in 1465 Domenico di Giovanni, landlord at Fontebecci, was convicted for the theft of a mule belonging to countess Caterina, the wife of the count Flaschi of Tiziano "lombardo". Those must be times when the hotel was not a safe place: the following year, Gherardo di Stefano di Alemania was convicted "for having subtracted from a hotel at Fontebecci an axe and a big kitchen knife" worth 40 *soldi*.

In Fonte Becci there was another receiving structure, functioning as inn and hotel, belonging to the hospital of Santa Maria della Scala.

The itinerary continues on the Chiantigiana, on another ridge with beautiful landscape openings. After less than one kilometre, on the left, is the villa of

Montarioso

Today the seat of the Regional Seminary, it housed the Museo Diocesano until 1995 (now being transferred into the Oratory of San Bernardino in Siena). The XIX century villa was built by the Vecchi family, three storied and with a tower, on a square plan. The front is divided into three strips, in Renaissance style, alternating a fake rustication at the base, a lighter rustication above and smooth plaster on top.
From the Chiantigiana we detour again, turning at the sign to Basciano on the left. After about 400 metres, on the left is the

villa Parisini

"It seats on a flat hill at the entrance to Chianti, on the left slope of the river Staggia. The most ancient memory I know, referring to this place, I have found in a public donation confirmed in the year 812 in favour of the monastery of St Bartholomew of Pistoja, to which three farmhouses located in a place called Basiano ... in finibus Senense *were assigned."*

A compound dating back to 1750, when Cavalier Giovanni Sansedoni decided to enlarge a rustic structure, belonging to his mother's family; a century later, in 1847, the proprietorship passed to the Parisini family. In 1961 the Sienese *Amministrazione provinciale* bought it from the Parisini heirs. Most probably, the design must be ascribed to the Florentine architect Giovanni Marchetti, who also designed the oratory. The compound includes various

agricultural buildings (the granaries, the barn, the hut, the wine warehouse). The harmonic relationship of the buildings with the surrounding vegetation bears a particular significance: the Italianate garden laid out in two sectors on the front, the "romantic" thicket on the back. The division of rustic spaces also responds to a strict hyerarchic order, extending from the most dignified building to those exclusively devoted to agricultural uses. The architectural scheme of the villa is based on typical Renaissance style: on a square plan, it is divided in two orders and the attic. On the façade, embellished by pictorial decorations, a three-arched porch is repeated on the upper storey. In the interior decoration, the villa expresses synthetically the artistic taste of the time, linked to a lifestyle which preferred the isolation of the country side as a stimulus to reflexion and the search for a virtuous life, symbolized by the ceaseless search for the classic world as a form of existential balance. A flight of steps starting from the hall on the ground floor leads to the first floor; inside the walls of the central hall, on the first floor, decorate by a rich collection of ancient busts, almost a gallery of sculptures, in line with the love for antiquities typical of the XVIII century. The twenty busts, in white Carrara marble, are distributed on three rows; they stand on scrolled stucco corbels, or are inserted in niches with stucco decorations. The collection includes a series of the twelve Caesars, a subject very much in demand at the time and circulated through copies, in which we can recognize three portraits of Domitianus, Nero, two ellenistic busts portraying women, the portraits of Faustina and Lucretia and one of an amazon, besides the head of an old man with a vacant stare, maybe an image of Homerus. On the first floor, we enter the main hall from the portico: the ceiling is decorated with grotesques, and the walls are in Pompeian style, in line with the fancy for the antique world visible all over the building: other decorations include stylized vine-leaves and female dancing figures (the Muses?). The decorations of the adjacent rooms bear an echo of Baldassarre Peruzzi's style (a keen divulger of the grotesque decorating motif in the Sienese area), alternating *grisaille* patterns on gilded, red and blue backgrounds. The large marble panels, now empty, originally contained, in all probability, paintings by the Florentine artist Francesco Gambacciani (the author of the altarpiece in the adjacent oratory).

The oratory, designed by Giovanni Sansedoni around 1750 and realized by the architect Giovanni Marchetti in 1794, is adjacent to the villa. The interior, on a square plan, preserves a beautiful floor of variegated marble: the coat of arms of the Sansedoni family is enclosed in the centre. In the middle of the vault is the large canvas representing *The Trinity*; nearby, the smaller *Putti with the symbols of Passion*. Traditionally attributed to Antonio Nasini, in spite of their precarious conservation the paintings reveal in fact the felicitous hand of the baroque artist. The conventional religious subject are rendered with an emphathically rich brightness, mindful of Luca Giordano's influences. The three panels above the doors depict episodes from the *Life of the Blessed Ambrogio Sansedoni*, the modest work of an artist who uses the acronym F.F. (it could be Francesco Feliciati, a late eighteenth century painter, the son of the better known Lorenzo).

After the villa we continue for one kilometre until

Basciano

The toponym Basciano already appears in a document from the VIII century and, according to local tradition, it traces back to "Bessa" (from which Bessano), the name of a Roman general fighting against Totila's army. The original church was enclosed with the walls of the ancient castle, damaged during the transit of Arrigo VII's troops in 1313. The parish church was never prosperous: nearly in ruins, it was built again in 1736 (as remembered in the plaque placed at the entrance to the church). In 1801 it received the title of Pieve. The building is dedicated to St John the Baptyst; the exterior was restored in neogothic style at the beginning of this cen-

tury. The façade is in red brickwork, and the portal is surmounted by an ogive arch. Inside, the most ancient work of art is the fresco on the left wall, depicting *St John the Baptyst*, recently ascribed to the Sienese Bartolo di Fredi, and dating back to the end of the XIV century. The painting, particularly elegant in the flowing lines and in the accuracy of the features, openly hints to the sophisticated style of the gothic painting of the beginning of that century, from Simone Martini to Lippo Memmi. In the atrium is a tryptich, the restoration of which has a peculiar story. It is a rectangular board, divided into three partitions, until a few years ago revealing the identifiable stylistic traits of Alessandro Casolani. After a restoring intervention in the Sixties, with the removal of XVI century layer, some figures stylistically close to Pietro degli Orioli came back to the surface (unfortunatley in bad condition): the unidentifiable saint on the left and the Virgin with child in the centre; the Casolanesque saint on the right was preserved. The terracotta statuette representing *St John the Baptyst*, in the baptysmal niche in the chapel on the left, reveals echoes of Sansovino's XVI century sculpture.

We go back now on the Chiantigiana, proceeding in the direction of Castellina in Chianti until

modern suburb of Siena, belonging to the territory of Monteriggioni on the left handside of the road only: the rest is in the territory of Castelnuovo Berardenga. Behind this administrative peculiarity lies a morphologic condition: the ubication of the settlement on top of the hill ridge on which, on the border with the Chianti region, runs the Strada Statale (state road) 222 called "Chiantigiana". This position, remarkable for the evocative landscapes, played in the past an important strategic role: a trace of this is the tower enclosed in a group of country houses, and the ruins of a wall, visible following the sign just before the end of the village, where the road makes a sharp bend. These are the remains of an important castle, which, preceded by Monteriggioni and followed by Aiola, Selvole and Pievasciata, formed a Sienese "medieval Maginot Line" against the Florentine threat.

After Quercegrossa we continue on the Strada Statale 222 "Chiantigiana" leaving it by taking a gravel road on the left (sign to Lornano), passing through vineyards, to reach a tarmack road again at Quattrostrade. Here we continue on the left, passing by the settlement of Topina and reaching

About 90 family used to live in the Quercegrossa castle at the beginning of the XIII century. Between 1210 and 1214, the castle was bought by the comune of Siena, at the time of the building of Monteriggioni.
On May 22, 1230, the Florentines trespassed the Chianti borders towards Siena, burning and ramsacking the castles on their way: but not the Quercegrossa one, which, according to Davidsohn, "was amply provided with glass containers full of Greek fire". Defensive resources and imperial prohibition, though, did not prevent the Florentines from conquering and destroying it two years later, in the month of June. "Quercia Grossa thanks to that event was object of utmost importance to the comune of Siena, which, through a representative, lodged a complaint to the imperial court situated in the Sienese territory, as it appears from the accusation of June 1232, and from the conclusions of the fiscal lawyer following after the peremptory deadline commanded to the Florentines, who were to appear in court before Halloween, least they should pay a 110,000 silver *marche* to the tax offices, and of 600,000 liras for the damage caused to the comune of Siena". The castle was subsequently rebuilt and was again, at least after 1260, an important borderline outpost, on the Chianti route towards Florence. Around 1374 the famous sculptor *Jacopo* was born here, and thus called *della Quercia.*

Lornano

Where a peculiar modern adaptation partially hides the perception of the church as a religious building: its foundation, dating back to the XI century, is nevertheless ancient. The church was born as an institution of the canons of the Duomo of Siena, at it gathered, at least until 1365, about ten prelates. It was damaged during the war of 1554, and declared unusable by the inhabitants in 1574. This was confirmed during the pastoral visit of the

cardinal Francesco Bossio, a year later: it was restored in 1576. The present arrangement dates back to the XVIII century restorations: the bell tower was built in 1715 and, on such occasion, a room was built, to be used as the sacristy: until then, the priests were forced to wear their liturgical garments underneath the platform of the high altar. The whole bulding was renovated and enlarged between 1719 and 1726. In 1728 Alessandro Zondadari, archbishop of Siena, consecrated it. The high altar was erected in 1721; the side altars followed a few years later: the one on the left is dedicated to the Madonna of the Rosary; the one on the right to the Crucifix. In 17361 Giuseppe Nicola Nasini frescoed the apse, with *St John the baptyst pointing to Jesus and the Apostles in front of the corwds.* The paintings which embellished the inner façade are still in their original position: behind the baptysmal font, of 1727 is the *Baptysm of Christ*, a work by a Sienese XVII century painter (Bernardino Baroni?) and, behind the holy water basin, sculpted in the same year by Mazzuoli, is *Saint Anthony Abbot with two angels*, probably by Nasini himself. The stucco panels are by Domenico Rusticoni, as canon Merlotti informs us. In the square in front of the church a small tower is what remains of the ancient settlement.

from here, we continue towards the left descending to the 'Autopalio'. Just before the entrance to the freeway, a detour on the right takes us to the scenographic rural nucleus of

Campo di Fiori

composed in rural forms, enriched by steps and small loggias.

Just after the entrance to the Autopalio, on the left, a blind alley leads to the Poggio Orlando area, where there are a few, almost forgotten remains of a local quarry of sulphur, which lasted until the second world war: a splint of industrial archeology, constituted by a small nucleus of housings for the miners, and by the remarkable crystals of sulphur, chalk, aragonite still to be found in the area.

164

Back to the junction, we pass under the Autopalio continuing on the left, through the modern industrial settlments of Badesse. We then go beyond the river Staggia and we meet the road n. 119, the heir of the new Francigena. Right on the junction, behind a chapel with *cotto* decorations, we recognize the wall screen of the ancient Mulino delle Badesse (mill of the Badesse), formerly owned by the Sienese monastery of San Prospero. The endowment fund is stated in a 1473 contract: "houses, fifteen lots of meadows, with juniper thickets and some oak-groves for a total of 140 *staiori"*. Not only this. The document also mentions an interesting trend, later destined to end for the number of quarrels it caused: to use the sharecropping system also for the running of the mill. On one hand, in fact, the nuns appear obliged to provide all the implements that were necessary for the functioning of the mill; on the other hand, the contracting party committed himself to pay "half of what the mill will yeld".

From the junction, we continue to the right, on the Strada Provinciale 119 "delle Badesse" which will soon be gravelled, in the direction of Monteriggioni. At first we will follow the straight valley bottom, and then we will climb up again amidst solitary woods, until a crossroads: following the sign to Florence, we will return to the Cassia, and then to Monteriggioni, thus closing the circle of our itinerary. Those interested in minerals should, instead,

follow the sign to Siena: taking back to the Cassia all the same, but allowing first, detouring to the left, to visit an abandoned limestone quarry, where beautiful crystals of quartz are easily found.

Monks, artists and sharecroppers

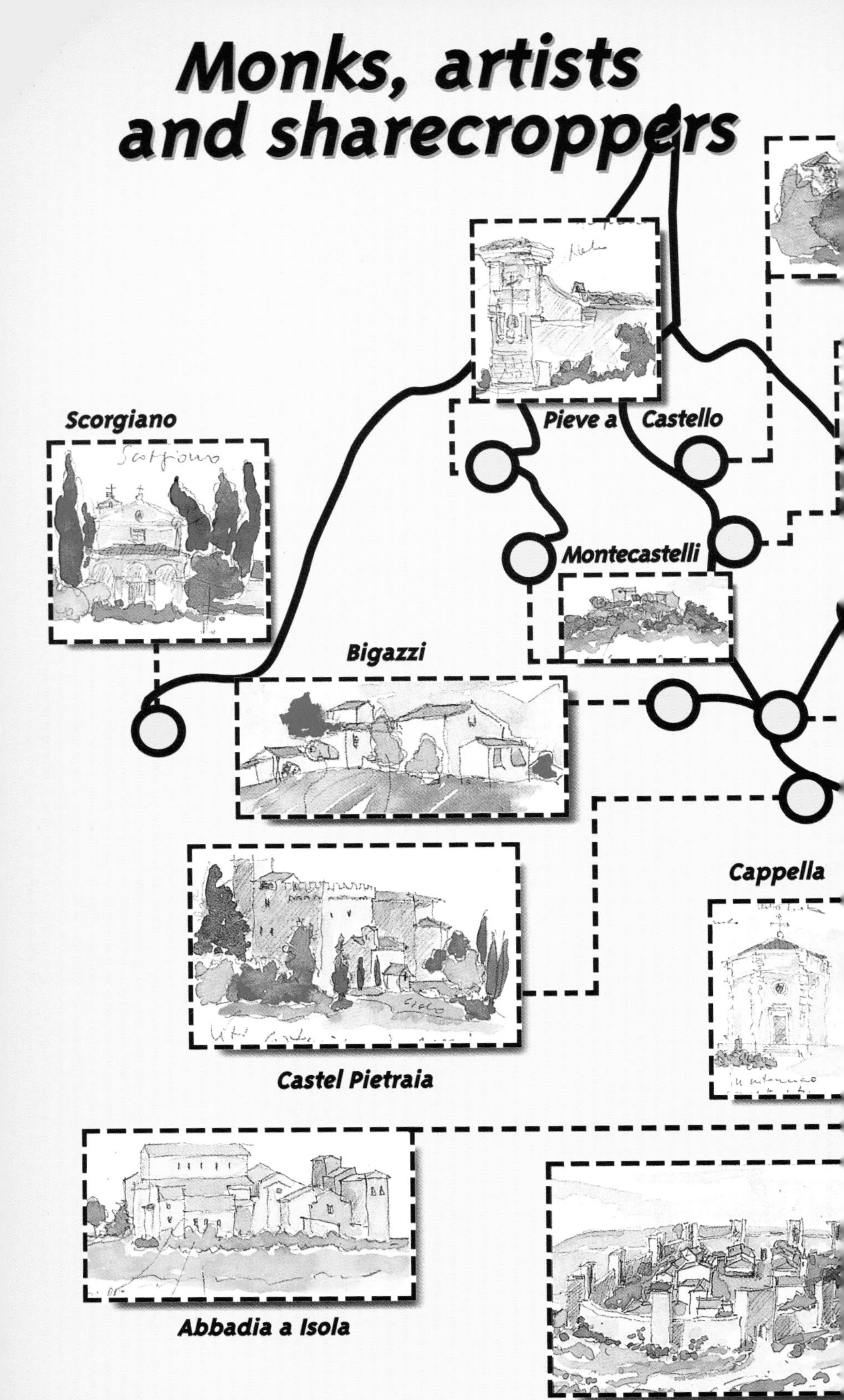

Second itinerary

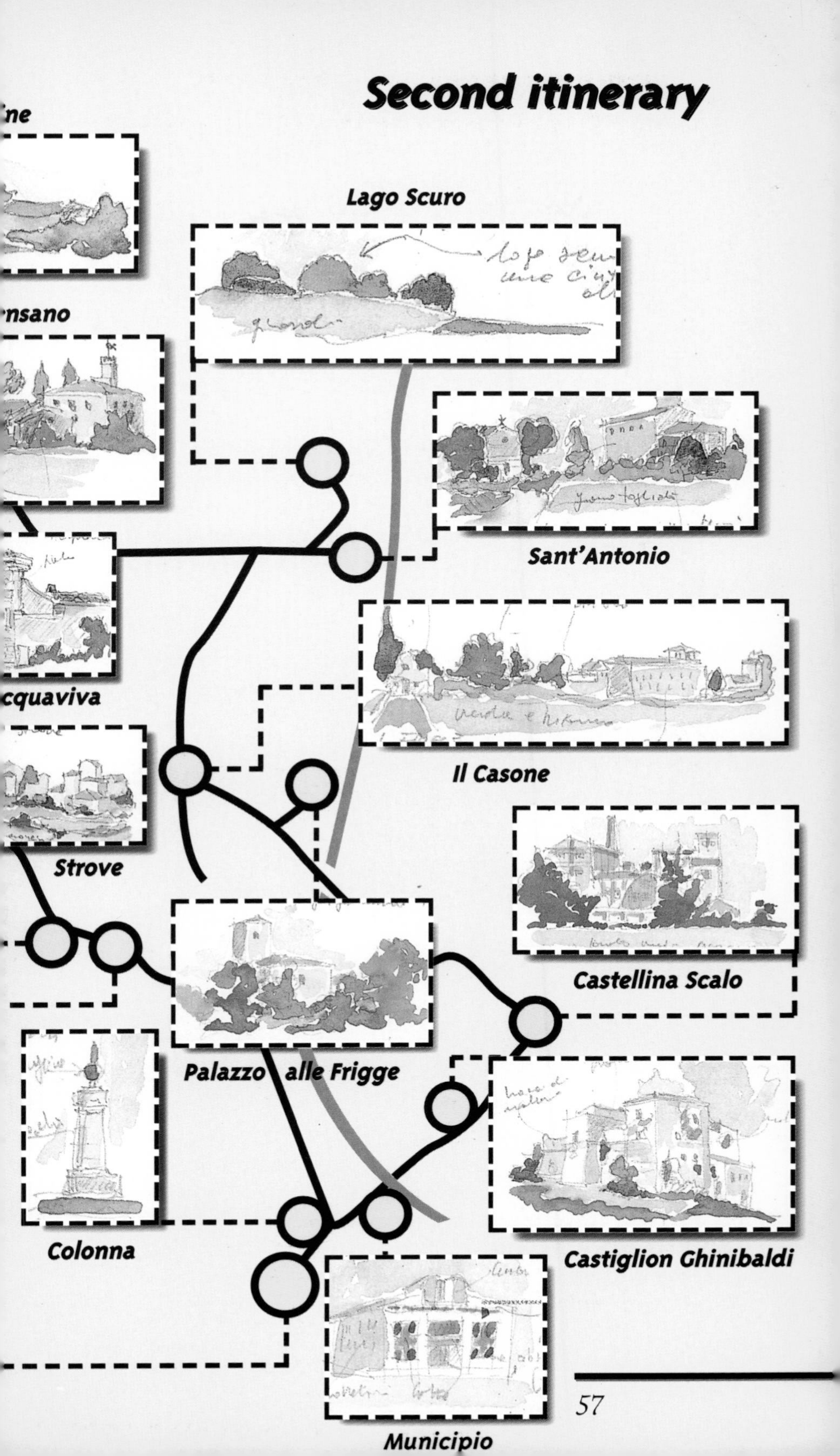

"Abbazia dell'Isola near Staggia at the eastern base of the Monte Maggio was called of the lake because of the swamps flanking it"

Abbadia a Isola

It is difficult to imagine today, instead of the fields surrounding the houses, the medieval marsh the hamlet stood out of, like an island, as the toponym confirms, and that played such an important role in its history.

176

Coming from the Strada Provinciale , "Traversa Monteriggioni-Casole", after having passed on the left the remains of some tombs, the north side of Abbadia a Isola appears like a hamlet clustered around a church with a tall central nave, while the aisle is mixed up with the roofs of some of the houses. There are no evident traces of fortifications on this side, and the eye can wander inside the hamlet, lingering among the stone houses and the narrow alleys.

171

Getting nearer along the road, we meet on our left a restored ancient well. Immediately afterwards, we see Abbadia a Isola from another perspective, which changes completely its appearance. This side has, in fact, two strong features giving an overall impression of separation and closing: the road and the walls.

The road divides the historical part, on the left handside, from more recent buildings situated on the other side and dedicated to modern commercial activities: a petrol station, a shop and club (Circolo A.R.C.I.) which works as a bar and a meeting place.
The road, element of separation between two worlds (ancient/modern, monuments/shops), lies at the origins of the foundation of the Abbey, at the beginning of the X century (February 4, 1001). The site was chosen by Ava, a noblewoman of Longobard origins, and by her children, for the building of an abbey, precisely for the fact that it was on the route of the Via Francigena, the road leading to Rome from San Gimignano and passing through Siena. Once left the car in the space in front of the petrol station and the shops, oppoiste us is a building which prevents us from catching sight of the internal part of the ancient hamlet. It a long, whitewashed building; the roof, the shutters at the windows, some clothes hanging out to dry, the drain-pipes all contribute to delineate the image of a house. Only by a closer inspection, investigating the de-

176
154

tails, can we detect, beyond the architectural structure, in the curvilinear walls, the town-planning mark of the fortified hamlet, in which the houses followed the geometrical pattern of the fortifications, now partly destroyed.
To get a wider vision, we must leave the service area and climb up the road for a few metres, along the side of the old ditch. Here we find an ancient circular building: a tower, partly hidden by wall-creepers. With the finding of the walls, the ditch and the tower we have gathered a first series of elements allowing us to reconstruct/imagine on that side, the fortifications built to protect Abbadia - like so many other villages in the Sienese territory - from the mercenaries ramsacking the scarcely defended countryside.
Passing beyond the old gate in the walls, the evocative façade of the church of the saints Salvatore and Cirino stands up before us. Here we begin our visit.

The façade displays a whole series of modifications and adaptations, showing the complexity of the historical events which contaminated its previous unity. In fact, the façade as a whole, with a travertine coat, appears divided in three plans. In the lower part the original double portal was substituted by the only central opening; in the central strip, two side wings (of which, only the left one is authentic) are surmounted by suspended arches; in the upper part, two mullioned windows open up at the sides of the central round window; the front is decorated by blind arches. The little arches are decorated by a zoomorfic frieze and stand on corbels carved as human heads or rosettes.

On entering the building, the image before us appears as more homogeneous, in spite of the many interventions throughout the centuries. The building, on a basilican plan, has three naves each terminating in an apse, with a hammerbeam roof.
Large columns alternate with ribbed pillars; the parallelepiped bases are joined to the columns by a simple band; the only carved capital, with two human praying figures dressed in Roman clothes, is the one on the half-comlumn separating the central apse and the smaller apse on the left.

The abbey at Isola, as mentioned above, was founded in 1001 by Ava, from the noble family of the Lambardi, the lords of the area, and was endowed with a large allowance to secure its economic autonomy. The choice of the site was linked to the near Via Francigena, and the moanstery could also function as a hostel and give assistance to the pilgrims on their way to Rome.
In the course of the following century, the abbey consolidated its control on the neghbouring territory by acquiring lands and castles. In the mid-twelfth century, the monastic structure was already broadly developed, and furnished with fortified walls; the building of the romanesque church, consecrated in 1173, is probably to be placed during this phase.
Its position on the border between Siena and Florence exposed the church to a situation of continuous political and military tension. However, this did not compromise the economic stability of the monastery. Decadence, a phenomenon spread all over the Monteriggioni territory, began in the XIV century. Black Death at first, and wars later, caused a decline in population. The abbey, for its important military position, was fortified in 1376, at the expense of the *Comune* of Siena, and again restored in 1416. Nevertheless, the crisis became more severe: in 1445 the surviving monks were moved to the monastery of Sant'Eugenio near Siena, and, of the whole compound, only the church still functioned as a parish church.
From the end of the XIX century various interventions healed the partly decaying structures of the church, also heavily altering its general appearance. The intervention in the Fifties eliminated also the XVIII century bell tower, in the fear that its weight might compromise the stability of the structure.

Starting from the end of the XIV century, various mural paintings were commissioned for the church of Isola: the *Madonna with Child, the saints John the Baptyst, Nicholas of Bari, Anthony Abbot, Catherine of Alessandria* was painted by Taddeo di Bartolo perhaps in the last decade of the century. With the evident hint to the gothic tradition of the beginning of that century, Taddeo stresses further his essential fidelity to Simone Martini's gothic models, marked here in the general linearity of the composition, although made heavier by more compact lines.

The **baptysmal font** placed at the beginning of the left wall dates back to the concession of the title of *pieve*, that is to say a church in which the believers could be baptysed, in 1409: on the moulding is carve the inscription GREGORIUS DEI GRATIA ABBAS HOC OPUS FECIT FIERI (Anno) I (Incarnationis) MCCCCIX.

The alabaster basin is palced on pillar decorated with geometric and fitomorphic carvings; in the five sculpted compartments the *Baptysm of Christ* is in the center, between two escutcheons of the abbey; in the compartments

at the two sides a *Bishop Saint* and a *Martys Saint* are represented. The unnkown author if the sophisticated scultpure seems to hint -in the intensity of the scene accentuated by the *chiaroscuro* - to Giovanni Pisano's language, rich in pathos, renovating it in the more gentle and gracious figures of the angels, clad in late-gothic garments.
At the beginning o the XVI century, another phase in the decorative cycle of the church was commissioned to Vincenzo Tamagni, a painter active in Siena and San Gimignano after his apprenticeship in Rome. The large fresco on the left wall, representing the *Assumption of the Virgin*, is unfortunately scarcely appreciable due to its precarious conservation. Here the artist revives iconographic themes and schemes widely tried out since the end of the XV century, limiting himself, with scarce origi-

nality, to the repetition of already experimented formulas. The tangible influences of Girolamo del Pacchia seem frozen here in the stunted landscapes and in the failed attempts to deepen the perspective. At the sides of the central scene are the *Blessed Ambrogio Sansedoni, Saint Bernardino Saint Sebastian.*
The whole figure of *San Biagio*, frescoed on the left wall, must be ascribed to the same artist for the evident analogies in the features of the characters.
One of the foremost examples of Sienese painting towards the end of the XIII century, the *Madonna enthroned with the Child and angels,*, now preserved in the Museo Diocesano in Colle Val d'Elsa, comes from this church. Recent studies on art in that period place it alongside with stylistic experiences such as those by the so-called "San Pietro Master" (author of an altarpiece in the Pinacoteca Comunale of Siena), in which Cimabue's language, clearly detectable in the composition, is interpreted through the experiences elaborated by the young Duccio in the 1280s while collaborating with the older master. An unknown painter, attracted by Duccio's innovative capacity to point the attention on the three-dimensional side of things, evident in the almost plastic structure of the throne. The polyptic by Sano di Pietro (1471) is a large panel divided in three compartments, with a lunette, pillars and a predella painted in 1471. It is considered one of the most successful works in the artist's ripe age. The intensity and elegance of the chromatic scale are accompanied by the lively freshness in the narration of the stories in the predella: the attention to the details in the ladnscapes and in the interiors is almost that of an il-

luminated manuscript. The sophisticated quality of the whole panel has been enhanced by the recent restoration, which also included the richly gilded and finely carved carpentry.

Inside the church, on the right wall is a portal surmounted by an architrave leading to the cloister and to the rest of the structures of the monastic complex, today in precarious condition. To get an overall view, we must exit the church and look over a gate situated on the right side of the building.

The settlement of the monastery appears, on the whole, as a structure which is both monumental for its dimensions, and complex for the architectural stratifications: the function the building was destined to changed often, altering its XI century benedictine connotation. At the beginning of that century, therefore before the church itself, the cloister had already been built (1062), while the monks' cells date to a few decades later (1110).

The oldest extant part is the eastern side, dating back to the XIV century, featuring a XIII century portico, on two storeys, with eight irregular brick arches leaning on capitals and columns probably rescued from another building. Next to stone columns are some brick ones, while some others are part brick, part stone. The portico area next to the church shows the rests of a bell tower, built in solid limestone blocks. The top is truncated where the roof of the church begins: the complex events in the history of both the church and the monastery often led to changes and different forms of use of the materials, especially in the decorative parts.

The abandoning of the monastery in 1446, and its subsequent destination as an agricultural structure in the XIX and XX century, modified some of the rooms according to their new function. The large cellars are located in two different spaces. The first, at the corner of the portico, displays beautiful tunnel vaults. In the second one, in the build-

ing in front of the portico, some masonry bar-
rels are preserved. These
are the most visible signs
of the changes in the
long run, when the same
structure turned from
religious dwelling into
an agricultural structure.
In the square, beside the
church is a chapel of the
Compagnia; an aban-
doned building with an
altar and traces of stuc-
coed decorations. In
front of it, the rectory.

177

At the beginning of the XII century the abbot of the benedictine monks, finally free from the tutelage of the founders, tried to liberate himself also from the obligations towards the bishop of Volterra, from whom he depended. He then asked the Roman Curia to free the abbey from the encumbrance by recognizing the ordination of the new abbot by the Pope and not by the bishop. The Roman Curia laid a condition for the acceptance of the request: the bishop of Volterra, in the past, must not have exercised his power in the election of the abbot during a period of at least thirty years. The answer was certainly not a casual one: in fact, there had perviously been an abbot, name of Rolando, who had led the community for over thirty years. Therefore, the bishop of Volterra could not have exercised his right for the time established by the Roman Curia.

From the church square, with our back to the façade, we turn right to continue our visit to the hamlet. After having passed by a door, feeble sign, together with a segment of the walls, of the ancinet fortification, we can go down a narrow alley and reach the lower part of the village, the first we caught sight when getting to Abbadia.

Nothing obstructs the view, extending on the whole plain until the hill of Monteriggioni. Continuing on the road, we get inside the hamlet again, under a stretch of solid walls. Turning left, and passing under a covered pasage, we get to a well-tended green spot. A track makes the crossing possible; thus we get to a wooden fence delimitating the end of the built area and the beginning of the cultivated fields.

The plain, Monteriggioni in the distance, and the woody slopes of the Monte Maggio offer a picturesque landscape, contrasting in colours and volumes. Inspite of this, it is worth our while to turn round and look towards the settlement.

An accumulation of different shapes, of heterogeneous materials stands before our eyes forming a very charming view. In particular, the contrast betwewen the square and regular stones of the restored apses of the church and the adjacent external wall of the monastery. The high wall presents a varied selection of building materials: stones alternate with red brick, used as a decorative pattern in the window frames and, although irregularly, also in the monastery wall. Externally, a stretch of the boundary wall, now totally hidden by wall-creepers, extends itself along the eastern side. It then makes a sharp turn and continues on the following side, surrounding the orchards, thus completing the complex of the 1376 fortifications.

From Abbadia we proceed towards Strove. Still inside the village, a few metres from the parking, we take a road on

the left and we go along it until an octagonal brick building, with stone ribs. The building differs from the neighbouring stone construction for the choice of the building material. There is little information about this chapel, which the locals remember as the church of the Lay Company of the Madonna of the Snow.

140

The Madonna of the Snow is related to a miracle handed down to us from a very ancient tradition. Pope Liberius, in the IV century, had decided to build an abbey dedicated to the Virgin; The Madonna intervend making snow fall in Rome in the middle of August, thus delimitating the space the church should occupy, and furthermore drawing the plan of the church with the snow itself. A beautiful church in Siena, inside which is a large altarpiece with predella by Matteo di Giovanni describing the event, is also dedicated to this miracle.

Just before the chapel, we catch sight of a water tank collecting the waters coming down from the Monte Maggio. In the Middle Ages, these small streams would cease flowing in the plain below, creating the marsh of the Canneto. Continuing on the gravel road, we arrive at the monument in memory of the partisans killed on the Monte Maggio. A little further on we get to Casa Giubileo, the country house where the battle took place, now Holiday Home and Didactic Centre.

140

In the middle ages many moments of the day were signalled by the bells. The bells could have played alerts tied to religion (such as the mattutino or the vespro) or to sudden dangers like fire or war or other tragical or happy events. The standard day was divided in a constant number of hours, part of a variable light-time (from dawn till dusk). In such manner an hour in winter was several minutes shorter than its summer counterpart. This depended on the little interest the middle ages men showed in measuring the abstract time, preferring the use of timespans based on natural events such as daylight and darkness. Therefore the time-measurement instruments were few and unreliable: among them we can quote the lasting time of a lit candle or the time a monk needed to read a cer tain number of pages.

The Strada Provinciale 41 "Traversa dei Monti", once left Abbadia, continues on a slight slope, alternating straight stretches to winding bits. After a few kilometres, on the left handside, not far from the road, we catch sight of a group of stone buildings. Among these, the church stands out, with a vaulted bell tower and a castle with battlements. It is Castel Pietraia, an ancient construction recently converted into flats.

Castel Pietraia

It was a large castle, transformed into a villa between the XV and the XVI century, with interventions almost completely eliminated by the last restorations. The framing of a door is all that is left of the Renaissance version. The original elements are today evident in the vast half-moon, with a scarp, in the adjacent tower and in the remains of another keep.
Continuing along the Traversa Monteriggioni-Casole, we immediately reach

Strove

"Strove in Val d'Elsa. Village, formerly a castle and contrada, from which the contrada -di-val-di-Strove took its name. It sits at the northern side of the Monte Maggio between the Pieve a Castello and the Abbey of St Salvatore a Isola.

The first architectural element before our eyes is the apse, with a stone bell tower, of a romanesque church. Getting closer, the rest of the settlement appears, with the round shape typical of the fortified hamlet. The remains of the walls are today scarcely detectable in the low walls surrounding the buildings in some points.

"I, Tegrimo son of Ava and Ildebrando, donate to Sinderada my beloved wife the fourth part of the tower, the castle, the hamlet and the countryside of Strove with the exception of the churcch of San Martino and its properties..." We are in the year 994, the emperor is Onorius II, the pope John II. Strove was afterwards one of the castles belonging to the Lambardi family, of Staggia. A large part of it was then passed on to the monks of the nearby Abbadia a Isola who, around 1123 would give it to the Soarzi family as feudal concession. The latter, on various occasions, alienated rights and properties of the castle to the *Comune* of Siena. The *Comune* finally took possession of Strove and of the neighbouring territory at the beginning of the XII century, keeping it until the fall of the Republic in 1554.

The visit can begin from the area in front of the church: a narrow green spot with a line of imposing cypress trees, bearing the slightly pompous name of *Parco delle Rimembranze*, donated in 1924, as reported in an inscribed pillar. The origins of the church of San Martino are thought to date back to the V century. The first mention of it appears in a dontaion act of 994, made by Tegrimo, Lord of Staggia, son of Ildebrando and Ava, the foundress of Abbadia a Isola.

The building, facing on the little square at the entrance to the village, has a sloping façade; the portal is surmounted by a lunette on top of which us a two-mullioned window (these last two details were added in the Thirties' restoration). The apse, decorated by tiers with a central mullioned window, is original; the walling is in rubble travertine.
The one-naved interior has a trussed roof; on the walls, alternating stripes of bricks and travertine create an effect of bicromy. The three present altars substituted the XVII century ones.

In 1087 the church of San Martino became the property of Abbadia a Isola. Priests from Strove are often mentioned as witnesses in many important documents of the abbey. With the expansion of the *Comune* of Siena, Strove, too, became a Sienese possession, and in 1215 the men of Strove took the vote of allegiance to Siena. In the second half of the XIV century Strove, like all the rest of the Monteriggioni territory, knew a phase of economic and demographic crisis; the emergency was overcome in the following centuries thanks to the increase in populaton. In 1937, the plaster was stripped off the walls, and the original internal walling came to the surface. Two niches were built, in which two new altars, in romanesque style, were placed.

In the one on the right is a *Virgin with Child.* The heads of the two figures are enriched by silver alos, while the rich frame is elivened by a series of panels where episodes from the Life of the Virgin are described, with quick strokes of the brush. A large arch on the left leads into the chapel of the Compagnia of the Santissima Annunziata, with a groin vault, and an XVIII century altar, sustained by a scrolled structure. At the sides of the altar are two beautiful ancient pews, reserved for the local authorities and the rector of the church; and two XVII century canvases representing the *Madonna with child and two Saints* (on the left) and *St Martin and the poor man* (on the right).

The most significant of the ancient ornaments of the church is the beautiful XVI century altarpiece, originally placed on the high altar and today preserved in the Museum of Colle Val d'Elsa. It represents *The Annunciation* and is signed and dated "ARCANGELUS SALIMBENI SEN. FECIT A.D. 1574".

Coming out of the church, walk down Via Matteotti. Shortly afterwards, on the left, we will meet a taller construction at present occupied by the hotel "Casalta".
Legend has it that this is the longobard church mentioned in the 994 document. Another remarkable building, with some archaic traits in the recently restored walling, is to be found at n. 4 of Via Gramsci. All over the hamlet it is possible to find interesting corners or walls. Today, the round planning of the buildings is the foremost proof of the origins of the hamlet as a castle; while at present, the most characteristic features of the village are linked to craftsmanship and agriculture. Today's image of Strove, quiet and orderly, has its contrast in the past, when the village was very lively, animated by a variety of actions

and a transit of jobs. In the alleys and in the squares the sounds and rhythms of the craftsman. Towards the fields and the woods, the presence of working animals - oxes, donkeys, horses - or cattle - goats, sheep, pigs. During celebrations the streets came to life thanks to the local band playing its music, while the last *Bruscelli* were performed, and the local amateur dramatic society put new plays on stage. Political life was also intense here: the *Casa del Popolo* (Home of the people, a left-wing enterprise) dates back to 1919.

27

The *Bruscello* was a form of theatrical performance in "eighth rhyme", acted out by male performers, dressed up as women when needed to. The themes would vary: epical enterprises, love fights, hunting. The plots always pivoted on a contrast between the characters: for example quarrels between father and daughter about the choice of a husband.
The term "bruscello" derives from the contraction of the archaic form "arboscello (small branch) and takes its name from the leading actor, which carries around a branch from a tree. The period of the performances was Carnival and Half Lent; the bruscelli were nevertheless staged also on other occasions, such as the fairs. The main square of the village or the farmyard were the stages. The "bruscellanti", on the fixed date, arrive in a pageant preceded by the musicians and stand in a circle.

On the back of the village of Strove a tarmack road goes to Acquaviva, an ancient hamlet around which are some modern houses. On the left handside is a Cross with the Symbols of the Passion, partly covering a "Madonnino" (tabernacle) with the Madonna of Provenzano. Up the road on the left is a small chapel. These are the silent sign of a different relationship with the sacred, in which also physical space was always permeated by the presence of God.

From Acquaviva we go back, to take again the Strada Provinciale 42 "Traversa Monteriggioni-Casole".

On country roads, it is still possible to meet shrines with religious images, particularly dedicated to the Virgin. This has led to the popular habit of calling these small constructions the "Madonnini". During the Reformation, the marian cult flourished, and numerous laical company were dedicated to it, like the one at Strove. In that cliamte was also born the cult of the madonna of Provenzano, related to a miracle by the Madonna occurred in Siena in the second half of the XVII century. A Spanish soldier shot an archibuse at the image of the Virgin placed outside a house. The Virgin was mutilated by the sacrilegious act and only the head remained uninjured. Since then, it started performing prodigies which caused a stir not only in Siena. The house where the image was hung was called "the house of miracles" and was transformed in a basilica. The July Palio is dedicated to the Madonna of Provenzano. The "madonnini" were mainly linked to the rite of the "rogazioni", rogations (rogare = to ask), a processional ceremony lasting three consecutive days before the Ascension. The priest, accompanied by the believers, would cross the country roads invoking the protection of the saints with special litanies. At the tabernacles, often adorned with flowers, he would stop and say prayers for the protection of the fields and of the harvest. After every route, which could last many hours, the priest would celebrate the mass. According to popular tradition, the "madonnini" would also protect the travellers from the evil spirits.

Bigazzi

On the other side of the road from Strove, on top of a hill, stands a complex building, recently restored, dominating the valley of Strove from its privileged position. Now private property and functioning as a hotel, it is what remains of the castle of Bigazzi.

Document proof its presence in 1318 as the castle of a local family, the ascendants of the Sienese family of the Montanini. Local tradition indicates this castle as the place of birth of Ghinibaldo Ghinibaldi, whose father was in fact at the service of the monks of Badia a Isola. Ghinibaldo, an important business man in Siena, is particularly remembered for his wife, Sapia, mentioned by Dante amongst the envious in the Purgatory, and who we will find later on at Castiglion Ghinibaldi.

100

The provincial road unwinds on the ridge of a number of hills. On the left are the beautiful landscapes of the western side of the Montagnola, gently sloping down into cultivated fields. On the other side is the plain of the Casone, until the middle Val d'Elsa, with the towers of San Gimignano in the background.
Along the road, on the left, is a restored country house, remarkable for its architectural structure. On the right, in rapid course, are two interesting setllements: "Sensano", presenting itself in its function of agricultural structure, with stratifications of agricultural buildings almost hiding the residential part. A little farther on is "Il Termine", hidden and protected by a barrier of cypress trees and by the thick vegetation of a garden.

This structure presents itself in its aspect of a villa, used as a summer abode by the owners, showing the different function of the farm . This spot on our route is particularly interesting for the quantity of wonderful constructions. As a matter of fact, on the right handside we soon meet a beautiful farmhouse, the massive body of which is made gentler by loggias on two sides. Its position on a ridge lets the eye wander towards particularly charming views: on the right a small, green pond surrounded by a vineyard a by a wood; on the other side a woody hill parallel to the ridge on which the road is, on top of which stands the old Montecastelli, now a little private hamlet. Behind is the settlement of Pieve a Castello, an ancient structure recently restored; The road passes by an ancient settlement, Rocca dei Monaci, developing on a hill on the left of the route. It is now a private structure, formed by a few buildings. The road continues downhill among dense vineyards on both sides.

We pass near an old abandoned chapel on the left. On the right is a farm with two old cement silos. We descend for a few hundred metres, until we reach the plain formed by the waters of the Elsa river, where the road forks. On the right is the bridge of Santa Giulia. Going along, it is possible to proceed either towards Colle Val d'Elsa (north-east) or climb up the high Val d'Elsa. On

The architecture of private villas, and also of some farmhouses in the Sienese territory, has been greatly influenced by the architectnic theories of Baldassare Peruzzi, one of the greatest Italian architects in the XVI century.
Brickwork, the typical material of the clayey Sienese territory, was used by Peruzzi to enhance the elegance of the constructions: the use of porticos on the ground floor is a typical example. On top of the porticos, loggias would be built, alternating empty and full spaces which gave the buildings both movement and lightness. This meant a radical change in comparison with the previous stoutness of residential homes. Besides architectures planned and realized by Peruzzi himself - among which is the Villa Petrucci at Santa Colomba - there are many farmhouses, built between the XVI and the XX century, which, like this one, follow the lesson by Peruzzi in the simple harmony of their lines.

115

the left, the Strada Provinciale di Montemaggio leads towards Scorgiano. We take this direction. The route, continuously alternating steep hills and rapid descents, crosses cultivated fields, and then penetrates the wooded slopes of the Montagnola. Passing by a junction on the right, we find, shortly afterwards and on the same handside, another gravel road leading to two interesting settlements dating back to the Middle Ages:

Pieve a Castello

"Castle (Pieve) in the valley of the Elsa. Destroyed castle with a church under the invocation of St John the Baptyst".

The Pieve di Castello in the Middle Ages was a hamlet born around a relevant religious settlement; it covered a large territory including thirtythree churches. Its importance was due to its position: it belonged to the diocese of Volterra and stood on the border between the dioceses of Siena and Florence. Today, it is difficult to think that Pieve a Castello, long since abandoned by its population, was not only in the Middle Ages, but even in modern times, a populated place, almost reaching two hundred inhabitants in the XIX century. The first document in which the Pieve is mentioned is of 971; on the occasion of an exchange of lands between the bishop of Volterra and a private citizen. Many are the documents in which the Pieve is mentioned. The emperor Corrado II stopped here in the XII century; during that period the Pieve made an attmept at extending its rights thus absorbing the romtory of Montemaggio near Abbadia a Isola, without succeeding. Besides its important religious function as a pieve, it also performed legal functions, assuming a particularly important role in that area, which gave it a certain prosperity.
During the second half of the XIV century decadence crept in, because of the plague and of the wars between Siena and florence. The situation became so dramatic that the baptismal font was moved to Abbadia a Isola in 1409.
Repetti indicates an increase of the population in modern times. The 94 inhabitants of 1694 became 170 in 1745, 183 in 1833. After 1950, with the crisis in agriculture and

the end of the sharecropping system, the church and the village were abandoned. They were then bought by privates and totally restored in recent times.

The church, dedicated to Mary, is now being recuperated with the rest of the ancient hamlet. Originally, the structure had a three-apse plan, with a hammerbeam roof. The simple façade, vastly altered, has a portal with a round window above. The north side bears traces of the two arcades which, in the romanesque version, substituted the four of the original basilican structure. The well-preserved

apse has pilaster strips above which are two suspended arches with brick finishing. Inside, the church preserves the classical appearance it gained after the 18th century remodelling. The walls are plastered, with a hammerbeam roof; on the sides are two large windows. A lancet arch once led from the right aisle into the baptistry, on a central plan, detectable on the outside because of the octagonal perimetre.

Continuing along the gravel road, beyond the Pieve di Castello, we climb towards the top of a hill, a private property, where are some farmhouses now restored. In particular, the most northern one mantains some traces of the ancient castle: the door and some arched windows. This is what remains of the old

Montecastelli

In the XII century it belonged to the Soarzis, Lords of Staggia, and is mentioned together with MonteMaggio in the various donations the Soarzis made to the bishop of Siena. At the end of the XII century, an agreement between the Soarzis and the abbey of Abbadia a Isola established that no building would be built without the abbot's consent. Nevertheless, Abbadia, too, was subject to pressures by Siena: thus, to strenghten their rights on Montecastelli, besides Monte Maggio and the marsh of Canneto, the monks concocted a fake imperial document, signed by Henry VI, ratifying the rights of the Abbey on the aforementioned territories.

From Monte Castelli, we go back along the gravel road until the junction with the provincial road we had previously left on our detour to Pieve a Castello and Montecastello. After a few kilometres, the road makes a more definite turn towards the Montagnola, entering a mediterranean bush with oak trees, holm-oaks and pine trees, and then climbs steadily up alternating straight bits to some bends. After a few kilometres, the road turns to the west, leaving the wood and running parallel to the ridges of the Montagnola. Some vineyards, a sign of the nearby farm of Scorgiano, line the road.

Scorgiano

"In the village of Scorgiano the noble folks of Staggia and Strove had their lordship [...]. Later on, the village of Scorgiano together with Montagutolo del Bosco, Pieve a Castello and other possessions, was made into a domain with the title of county by the Grand duke Ferdinand II, who, by means of a diploma in date May 11 1667, gave permission to the squire Giovanni of the late Firamno Bichi from Siena, to pass after his death to Cardinal Antonio Bichi, his brother [...] until at the death of the count Francesco of Firmano Bichi, which took place on September 7 1737, the feud of Scorgiano returned to the grand-ducal crown".

The ownership stayed in the hands of the Bichi Borghesi long afterwards, until, once the male branch of the family was extinguished, it became, through the female line, the property of the Brini family.
Today, Scorgiano appears as a complex structure including a villa and farm, closely linked and enclosed by one

boundary wall. An Italian garden precedes the villa, a building of simple and dignified elegance continuing, on the sides, into the mews. These spaces are interesting for the care given to the details and for the choice of materials. The horse-ponds and the troughs above them appear as jewels of furnishing. Behind the villa is the farm. It might be slighting to define the set of buildings as a farm, but it is useufl to give sense to the function of the agricultural organization to the whole structure, which includes

cellars, granarys, warehouses and workshops. Outside the villa-farm of Scorgiano there are only a restaurant, a private construction and a chapel, erected by the cardinal to celebrate the title and the estate.

Coming from Scorgaino we retrace our steps. Once arrived nera the bridge of Santa Giulia, we meet a junction, where we go to the right, along the Strada Provinciale 42 "Traversa Monteriggioni-Casole". After a few hundred metres, we turn to the left on the Via della Cerreta, a gravel road taking us to the Strada Provinciale "Volterrana". We then turn to the left again, on a gravel road ending in the Strada Provinciale "Volterrana".

The route runs along short straights and curves in a succession of woods and cultivated fields. The vast horizons of the previous bit along the ridge now give way to more secluded and definite visions. The road continues until it gets near a wood on one side. Shortly afterwards, on the right is the wide, tree-lined drive of a villa: we can see its façade in the distance. Continuing, we get to a junction with the Volterrana road, which takes to Colle on the left, and to Monteriggioni on the right. ➛ 94

Alternative route to Sant'Antonio del Bosco

Taking the road to Colle, after a few kilometres, on the right hand side we find a gravel road with a sign to Sant'Antonio. Following it we encounter two small lakes, the Lago Chiaro and the Lago Scuro, a small church: Sant'Antonio del Bosco, and an ancient monastic structure.

148

Various legends "explain" the singularity of the lakes in the highland of Sant'Antonio. One of them was oublished at the end of last century by the geologist Pietro del Zanna. "According to a legend which we find mentioned in an ancient chronicle, preserved in the Pieve of Staggia, Sant'Ambrogio, on his way to Rome, stopped at an inn on the old *maremmana* road to spend the night there. In the evening, as he was recovering from the labours of the journey, he entertained himself talking familiarly with the landlord; the latter, telling about himself, said (rare case) he was happy, with no desires and that no misfortune had ever upset his serene contentment. On heraing such words, the Milanese bishop ordered his escorts to get ready for a prompt departure, as an immense disaster was threatening that house. In fact, the saint man with his retinue had just left, when the house collapsed with adjacent grounds, and waters collected in the abyss forming a lake". More than three centuries before, the legendary aura surrounding the lakes ahd not escaped the attention of Leanrdo Alberti, renowned scientist and traveller. In his *Descrizione di tutta l'Italia* (Description of Italy) he wrote: "Near the Abbadia, honorauble country situated between the boundaries of Florence and Siena, are two lakes, within an arrow's shot of each other. In one of those the water is clear but the bottom can't be found (as the locals say), while in the other one (much smaller) the water appears so dark that it can be compared to ink. And the nature of this water is totally opposite to that of other waters, as if a piece of wood is thrown in it, it sinks in the depths, and can't be seen any longer. And fish can't be found here. It is widely known among the inhabitants that as Saint Cerbone the bishop of Massa was passing by, and stopped here to rest (where the first lake is), where an inn was, and realizing the life of vice that the landlord led, and intenting to make him repent from his sins, and judging he could not convert him, on the following morning he declared that the landlord and his inn would sink into the abyss, and that as soon as the bishop left, the grounds opened up swallowing the building, and the said lake was left in its place. Of the other lake, they say that a wicked sodomite lived here, and having lived in such wickedness for very long, God did not want to bear with him any longer, and made the grounds open up and made him sink with all his family, leaving this lake of the blackest water and of an opposite nature to other water, inasmuch as his house was".

Hermitage of Sant'Antonio del Bosco

"Situated in between two little lakes, reamindeгs of an older, wide marsh, about a mile from Abbadia a Isola"

such is Repetti's entry, linking the religious settlement with the two small water basins. The hermitage of Sant'Antonio al Bosco, or Heremus of Silvamaggio, is documented since 1245 as an augustinian monastery. In the XVI century, a convent was built on the site of the monastery, inside which is an ample cloister with a portico.

Church of Sant'Antonio

At the end of the XIX century, the small church in mock romanesque style was built, using material from the ancient monastery. The structure has two naves. The walling does not appear as original, while the little portal on the left, with a lunette and a round arch, together with the ashlars at the base of the apses and the marble coat of arms inside the lunette of the main portal, seem authentic. Uncertain is the attribution of the spire on the façade.

91

Retacing our steps from Sant'Antonio del Bosco, we get back to the junction with the Volterrana, where we came from.
We go towards Monteriggioni, noticing on the left the lateral block of a villa, the façade of which we had caught sight of from the drive. Next to it is a small chapel. on the side, closer to the road, is a rectangular building, the side walls of which are capped by a series of spires holding stone spheres and terracotta cones. It is the villa's *limonaia*.

The *limonaia,* together with the fish tanks, is a typical feature of Tuscan villas. It was the place where, in the cold months, delicate ornamental plants were kept. The buildings often featured large glass windows. Although their main function was a practical one, they soon became a furnishing of the garden. The plants were kept in earthenware bowls that should be large in order to let the roots expand, but not too much, so that they could still be easily handled when moved inside during the winter. The job of extracting and/or putting back the bowls in the limonaia was a delicate one, as it was necessary to forecast the weather: a night frost could damage the plants. It was, moreover, a trying task, as it involved the effort of moving plants of large size, cast in big earthenware bowls filled with soil. The plants were mostly used to decorate the space in front of the villa; their appearance marked the beginning of the warm season.

Starting in the XIV century, on the towers of town halls mechanic clocks were placed to indicate to everyone the time of the day. the passage to this new way of measuring time and its diffusion does not only represent a techinical innovation, but indicates also the birth of a new mentality, which considers time as an element that must be dominated. For the merchants, time is money. The interest, from this point of view, is not only an economic category, but an attempt to make time one's own, using it for one' own profit. The time elapsing between a loan and its restitution, representing the premise for the interest, is taken by the merchant as his own goods. In vain will the Church in the Middle Ages attempt to contrast this "human appropriation of time". Mechanic clocks become the symbol of a new concept, and the presupposition for radical changes.
With the mechanic clock, natural time, that is to say dominated by metereological elements (light and darkness) disappears. Moreover, the internal rhythms, once based on the succession of the sacred and the profane, experience a dramatic change, based as they are on regular, neutral intervals, filled by man according to a convention.
The interesting element of this item is the existence of the clock (town time) alongside with the bells (the old natural time).

On the left handside of the road, we meet first a decaying devotional chapel, and then the long block of a building surrounded by a wall, called il Casone. The central part is surmounted by a turret bearing a clock. On top of it is a bell with a hammer. The boundary wall around the park makes a right angle where it meets a narrow road leaving

the Volterrana in the direction of Colle. Nearby is the podere Taverna, a toponym deriving from its previous function as a receiving structure (*taverna* means inn).

After a period in wich people where hosted for charity, from the half of the XIII century, new hosting on payment structures begun to raise. Expecially in the city the big merchant family, like those of the Marzi or Malavolti, became owners of important hotels. Near the hotels begun to raise the inns, hosting structure far more modest, composed of few rooms on the ground floor.
Usually the inn was composed of a refectory, a kitchen and a store, situated under the basement, while at the first floor there were few rooms for the guests and the host's family. The bedrooms where in fact a single room that the customers shared, with straw mattress laying on the floor. Very famous is the novel by Sacchetti featuring a traveler who one morning wakes up in a inn bedroom and finds out that he shared the mattress with a dead man.
On the outside of the inn you usually could find a fenced area for horsekeeping.
Finally, the taverns were restoration structures where wine was sold and occasionally fruit. They where composed of a big central room, which contained some tables and a counter where you could buy black or white wine, and of a basement (*celliere*). On the counter where the wine measures and the wood or iron cups for drinking.

Shortly afterwards, we take a gravel road on the left taking us to

Palazzo alle Frigge

There is no historical information on this building, nor is its name explained. The structure reminds of the medieval *casa-torre*, a house in the shape of a tower, and the typical events following which, from being the master's house, it then slowly turned into a rustic residence. This structure has a charming outline when viewed from the Florence-Siena *superstrada*. On a hill, lower than the road, amongst the greenery is a tall medieval tower made of

blocks of stone, inserted in a stone farmhouse. From the road to Castellina, the vision is much reduced, as only the tower appears.

In the immediate vicinity, many archeological finds were dug out: tombs of various tipologies, easily recognizable, dug in travertine, a series of the *colombario* ones, turned into hen-houses by the peasants' DIY., in the recycling mentality intrinsic to rustic poverty.

The area is rich of findings from the past. Between Palazzo alle Frigge and the nearby Sant'Antonio, the most remote demonstrations of human activity in the territory of Monteriggioni were found: a rich collection of stone finds from the medium Paleolythic.

After having bypassed the Florence-Siena *superstrada*, we cross an industrial area and finally get to Castellina Scalo.

Castellina Scalo

This village first developed along a stretch of the Cassia coming from Poggibonsi. In the last century, the arrival of the railway gave its growth a further boost. In fact, both the road and the rail tracks constitute the axis around which the village defined itself in the course of time. Only

in the past ten years was a new guiding line created, along the sides of a slope in the western direction. Unlike most of the rest of the villages, which have at least partly preserved their medieval plan, Castellina appears as a modern settlement, where the speedy development did not allow the outlining of a definite town planning. A commercial centre with many shops, it possesses a few interesting buildings:

Church of Cristo Re

The Church of Cristo Re is of no relevant historical or artistic interest: it was built in 1933-34by the architect Severino Crott, in a mock byzantine style, of which a certain homogeneity is preserved, both in the external structure and in the interior ornamentation.

Greatly worshipped is a small coloured wooden sculpture, representing the Virgin with Child, probably of French school of the beginning of the XV century, placed on the left side of the transept.

Puccioni industrial plants

Other buildings of interest are the old Puccioni industrial plants, on the road leaving Castellina Scalo towards the junction with the road to Castellina in Chianti.
It is an example of industrial archaeology. The most interesting feature lies in the variety of forms of the buildings, apparently developing without any planning but revealing, in the contrast between the curved lines of the roof of a warehouse and the rigid vertical lines of the adjacent structure, surprising scenographic effects.

The proximity of the road and of the railway turned Castellina in a thriving commercial centre.

500 passengers a day and 15.000 animals: this was the traffic on the Siena-Florence post route, according to the calculations made in 1848 by special human "meters" placed night and day on the important artery. These figures, based on the current fares, made it possible to foresee a gain of 807.200 Tuscan liras to be made on the railway line linking Siena with Empoli, soon to be opened: the shares capital amounted to 10 million, therefore an 8% of yearly profit could be considered as a very good business. At that time, stagecoaches were still the fastest way to travel between Siena and Florence: 5 or 6 hours, choosing between the company run by Giuseppe Mazzarini, known as Geppetto, and that run by Ottaviio Lisi and partners. But, on June 10 1848, the *Strada Ferrata Leopolda*, the Leopolda railway, was opened: the first in Tuscany and third in Italy, making sure that Florence could count on a most efficient link with Livorno, now a port of international level. Siena could not afford being cut out of this new, central axis of communication.

STRADA FERR. CENTR. TOSCANA

ORARIO DELLE PARTENZE

DAL DÌ 28 MAGGIO 1860 FINO A NUOVA PUBBLICAZIONE

	I.	II.	III.
	ANT.		POM.
Parte da FIRENZE (Per la Leopolda)	6. 30	— —	5. 15
" LIVORNO	6. —	—	5. —
" PISA	6. 13	— —	5. 33
" EMPOLI	8. 15	— —	7. 15
" OSTERIA B.a	8. 25	—	7. 25
" CASTELLO	8. 45	—	7. 45
" CERTALDO	9. —	—	8. —
" POGGIBONSI	9. 30	— —	8. 35
Arriva a SIENA	10. 20	— —	9. 10
Parte da SIENA	10. 15	POM. 3.	— —
" ASCIANO	11. 15	6. 10	— —
" RAPOLANO	12. —	6. 25	— —
" LUCIGNANO	POM. 12. 23	6. 45	— —
Arriva ad ASINALUNGA	12. 45	7. —	— —

	I.	II.	III.
	ANT.	ANT.	POM.
Parte da ASINALUNGA	— —	7. 30	2. 30
" LUCIGNANO	— —	7. 45	2. 45
" RAPOLANO	— —	8. 5	3. 5
" ASCIANO	— —	8. 20	3. 20
Arriva a SIENA	— —	9. 30	4. 30
Parte da SIENA	6. —	— —	4. 45
" POGGIBONSI	6. 50	— —	5. 25
" CERTALDO	7. 10	— —	5. 55
" CASTELLO	7. 25	—	6. 10
" OSTERIA B.a	7. 40	—	6. 10
Arriva ad EMPOLI	7. 50	— —	6. 40
" FIRENZE (Per la Leopolda)	9. —	— —	8. —
" PISA	8. 25	— —	8. 15
" LIVORNO	9. 5	— —	8. 45

AVVERTENZE — Le Stazioni intermedie venendo chiuse appena giungono in esse i Treni, anche se questi anticipano, si raccomanda ai Signori Viaggiatori di prendere il biglietto 15 minuti avanti le ore approssimative indicate nell' orario.

Tip. di Onorato Porri

Taking the Cassia towards Monteriggioni, after about 800 metres we meet a detour on the right, signalled with a care inversely proprtional to its historical importance: the junction is, in fact, the heir of a most ancient receptive vocation. In the last century it was the site of a stage station for coaches on the Rome Florence route. In the Middle Ages, it was one hospital of the many along the Via Francigena and, in classical times, it was most probably a *mansio*, a stopping point. An authoritative and eloquent witness of these and other important events is

Castiglion Alto or Castiglion Ghinibaldi

standing above it, which is reached, from the junction, after 400 metres on a gravel road, the effort of which is made worth its while by the sudden discovery of an extraordinary fortified structure. Ignored, and thus protected from the close modernity of Castellina Scalo, its fascination is enhanced by its good state of conservation.
In spite of this, here is preserved one of the most significants archaeological findings in the whole territory: a square work, in small, regular travertine blocks, enclosed in the western side of the boundary wall.
It is impossible to retermine whether it is of Roman or Etruscan provenance, but it undoubtedly represents the surviving sign of the first urban settlement in the Monteriggioni territory: the "city of the living" joined to the "city of the dead" of the nechropolis of Casone, situated below.
During the Middle Ages, thanks to its excellent position, in control of the via Francigena, it was the seat of the castle and of the court of the Lambardi family, from Staggia. A part of it was then passed on to the bishop of Siena, and another to Abbadia a Isola. It was conquered and demol-

171

ished by the Florentines in 1158, and then rebuilt around 1230 by Ghinibaldo di Saracino, the husband of Sapia dei Salvani, made famous by Dante in the XIII chant of the Purgatory.
It then passed to the Salimbenis and, in the XVI century, to the Piccolominis: Francesco Maria, bishop of Pienza and Moontalcino, undertook various remodelling and enlarging. So many aouthors and different styles have, in fact, made Castiglion Alto a real architectural palimpsest. The basic XII century structure is detectable especially on the exterior sides, with roud corners on the south, west, and north sides. The east side is a XV century alteration: with a corner tower and a base with a stone framing on top. On this same side is the XVI century large portal, decorated on the top by two coat of arms (one of them, the Piccolo-

mini's) leading to the central court. The charm of the court, in state of abandon, is enhanced by the presence of remainders of the presence of country habits: a romantic contrast with the XVI century sophistication of the portico and of the two brickwork loggias, with basket arches and groin vaults.
The return of Castiglion Alto to an agricultural function recalls the origins of its most famous owner, Ghinibaldo, a rich landowner and the husband of Sapia, from the noble and powerful familiy of the Salvani. Not having had any male heirs, in 1265, shortly before his death, he founded a hostel at the foor of the castle, which by now bore his name. It was from the glacis of this castle that Sapia saw, rejoycing, the defeat of his

156 The hospitals started as a sort of benefit housing in cities and on main roads. In the sienese area of the "via Francigena" they were more then fourty. These 'hospitals' often depended on larger structures like the "Santa Maria della Scala" in Siena. The little hospital at Castiglion Ghinibaldi, like many others, had only four beds. The Monteriggioni hospital, a century later, counted just one bed. With the exception of particular events, such as an infective disease, the 'hospital' was mainly used as a night shelter for pilgrims. We know, from fifteenth century legal documents, that maybe the hospital of Castiglion Ghinibaldi later turned in an inn.

Sienese compatriots in the battle later called "of Colle". The fighting in fact took place in the nearby Sant'Antonio plain, situated below, on June 8 1269. Dante placed her, as an example of exasperated envy, in the livid landscape of the second cornice, hosting the sufferers from this vice:

«Io fui Sanese» rispuose, «e con questi
altri rimando qui la vita ria,
lacrimando a colui che sé ne presti.
Savia non fui, avvegna che Sapìa
fossi chiamata, e fui de li altrui danni
più lieta assai che di ventura mia.
E perché tu non creda ch'io t'inganni
odi s'i'fui,com'io ti dico, folle,
già discendendo l'arco di miei anni.
Erano i cittadini miei presso a Colle
in campo giunti co' loro avversari
e io pregava Iddio di quel che volle.
Rotti fuor quivi e volti ne li amari
passi di fuga; e veggendo la caccia,
letizia presi a tutte altre dispari,
tanto ch'io volsi in su l'ardita faccia,
gridando a Dio: Omai più non ti temo.»

Coming down from Castiglion Ghinibaldi, we take the Cassia southbound. Shortly afterwards, we get near Monteriggioni's town hall, built at the bottom of a hill.
Almost opposite, a road column indicates the possible three directions of a crossroads. Taking the road to Colle, we set on a logn straight crossing the western side of a fertile plain: it is the old marsh of Canneto. After centuries of work the marsh was drained of the waters that, coming down from Monte Maggio, stagnated there forming a sort of lake, thus forcing the via Francigena to follow the sides of the mountain, in an elevated position. The only traces left of the old marsh are the canals, crossing the plain, recognizable from the trees lining along them.
After about one kilometre, we leave the road to Colle and, turning left, take the Traversa Monteriggioni-Casole. Almost at the junction with the latter, on the left, where a small hill is, are some Etruscan findings. The road continues, quickly getting to Abbadia, where our tour started.

The ring of the lake

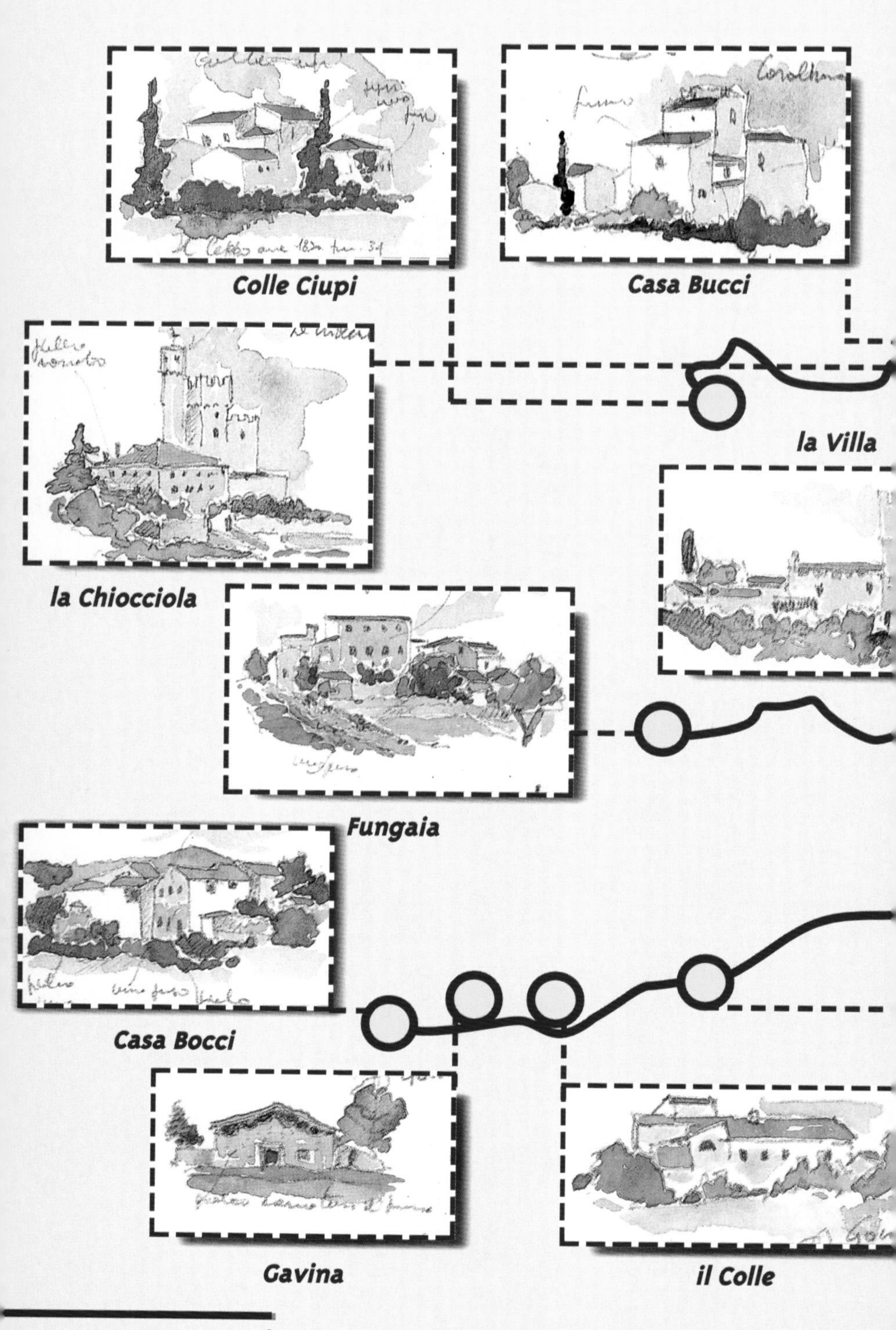

Third itinerary

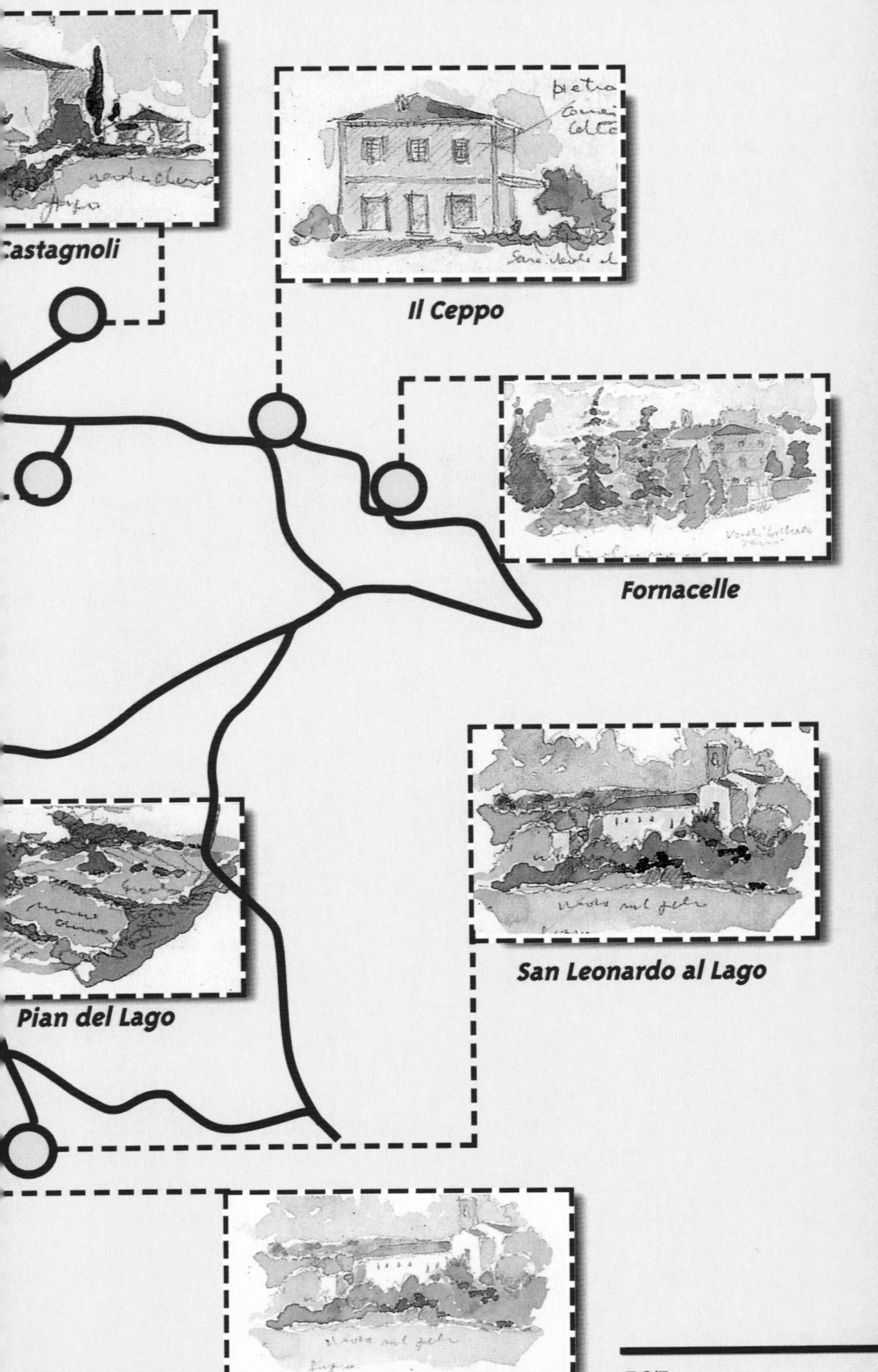

The route unravels along a ring, obliging us to to imagine the lake that used to occupy the meadows now faced by the villas, castles and monasteries dominated by the woods of the Montagnola.
The ring starts at the Ceppo, at the km. 235 on the Cassia Road, from which we continue towards Siena meeting on the left, after about one km, the

Villa di Fornacelle

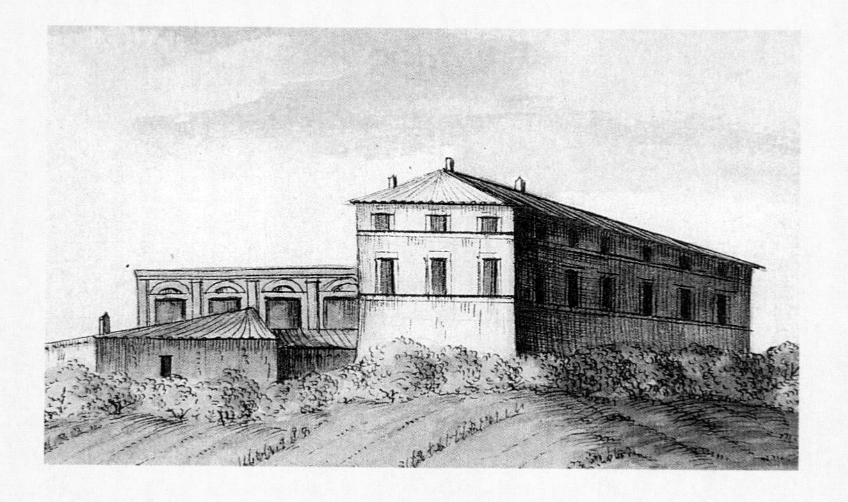

The building, recently converted in a compound of flats, dates back to the end of the XVII century, and used to belong to the noble Colombini; during the XVIII century it was passed on to the Testa family, and then to the Palmieri. The plan is in the shape of an "L"; on the plastered frontage is a blind loggia, reminding of the Peruzzi style, with rectangular windows; on the back, the façade has a fake portico with round arches framed by bricks, looking onto a large Italianate garden. In the XIX century some service buildings were added, such as the warehouse connected to the main block by a covered porch.

We continue on the Cassia, detouring on the right after 1 km. We ignore two more detours to the right, continuing to run along Pian del Lago: 1 km after La Fabbrica we detour on the right again, taking a gravel road from which, following the indication on the left, we climb on a road in bad condition, up to

San Leonardo al Lago

The hermitage is on the east side of the Montecagnano hill: its foundation dates back to the XII century, by a monk called Benedetto: the church already existed in 1168. The earls of the Ardenghesca, in the course of the XIII century, donated various lots o land to the monastery, and there was a remarkable land development towards Monteriggioni and Staggia. Starting from the middle of the century, up until 1516, the complex was united to that of San Salvatore a Lecceto. The two monasteries were both ubicated in an important territory, at the Siena borders: the "selva del lago", forest of the lake, became a strategical point of fundamental importance as it was a supply of energies for the city. The legend, linked to a fairy-tale interpretation of the Middle Ages, identified the forest as an inaccessible and harsh place, a refuge for the first christians, persecuted after the martyrdom of their first bishop, Ansano. In fact, that territory was populated and constituted an economical centre of some relevance, because of the incessant request for timber coming from Siena. The use of the woods was regulated by the Comune, which granted permission for its use and exploitation to the monks of the monastery. San Leonardo al Lago is the most ancient of the five monasteries that were founded at that time around the city (San Salvatore a Lecceto, Santa Lucia a Rosia, Santa Maria a Montespecchio, Sant'Agostino a Monticiano). At least at the beginning, it was not a hermitage, as it is quoted in the oldest documents as an *eccelesia*, church. The reputation of the monastery grew during the XIV century, when the Baeto Agostino Novello was attracted to its reputedly strict observation of the Benedictine rule, and stayed there leading a life of prayer and hermitage until his death, in 1309. The great influence the Blessed had on Sienese believers persuaded the monks to build a new church, embellished by paintings in the cloister in 1360, and ten years later in the apse, with the cycle frescoed by Lippo Vanni. In 1366 the monastery was fortified, to receive the population of nearby Santa Colomba in case of a war. In 1782, following the edict of Leopold, the Grand Duke of Tuscany, it was suppressed. It is now State Land, and is under the jurisdiction of the Soprintendenza per i Beni Ambientali e Architettonici di Siena. The ancient origins of the place are visible in the remains of the stone boundary wall, surrounding the hermitage, with the two towers, one square and one round, at opposite corners. The inside of the church has undergone radical transformations (the last restoration dates back to 1964). The bare appearance enhances with further efficacy the brilliance of the exhuberant colours painted on the walls of the choir by Lippo Vanni, in the representation of the *Life of the Virgin.* On the wall at the back, behind the altar, is the *Annunciation,* on the sides are the *Presentation to the Temple* and the *Wedding of the Virgin.* Crowds of angels playing musical instruments are painted in the four sectins of the vault, separated by ribs with a a trompe-l'oeil mosaic. In the entrance arch, in the middle, the *Assumption of the Virgin* is the remaining part of a vaster representation, which should have included the figures of the twelve apostles, today reduced to the group on the left. In the *piedritti* on the left, *San Leonardo* is depicted, above four episodes from the *Life of the saint* (three of them can be interpreted: *setting a prisoner free, the assistance to a tortured man during his inquisition, the liberation of a gentleman from an ambush by some bandits*). On the right is *Sant'Agostino*, below which is a depiction of the same *sant'Agostino praying with Santa Monica*. In the lower register is an inscription of difficult interpretation, in which the dates 1360 and 1370 appear, as a reference point for the dating of the paintings. These were found in the second half of last century under a layer of plaster that only partly revealed the four *Stories of San Leonardo.* The two large cycles on the walls are dominated by the architectural elements, functioning not only as a

setting, but also giving the scenes a theatrical formulation, almost trying to break loose of the limited space of the choir with prospectical expedients. The characters themselves are placed according to the architecture, underlining them in rigidly symmetrical schemes. The tribute to Ambrogio Lorenzetti's style, already evident in these scenes, is openly declared in the *Annucniation* , a tribute to the analogous representation by the painter in the church of San Glagano at Montesiepi. The intention of breaking through space is stated also in the festive crowd

Until the first half of the XVIII century Pian del Lago was deemed "perpetual enemy of Siena" because, as the mathematical Pietro Ferroni wrote "Between the hills of Lecceto and Santa Colomba the rain staunched thus turning to mud a huge plain that was just four miles far from Siena."
In such natural basin, that was partially dry during the summer and the first days of fall, the no longer submerged ground brought illness and disease to the city of Siena.
The convent of San Leonardo was often abandoned by its friars at the beginning of summer and reopened in the safe winter.
To tell the truth this swamp brought some good side effect. On its banks large grass fields allowed cattle breeding. Other useful resources were canes, leeches, firewood. Hunting and fishing were also well-developed.
Nearby the water level regulator a water mill functioned for several centuries. In the Biccherna books dating to 1226 we can find entries about payments for the maintenance of the lake's 'mouths'.
In 1262 the City Council of Siena issued some restrictions on fishing and gave the order to plant "in plano Silve de Lacu et in Valle de Rigo arbores et oppios et salices".

of the angels in the vault, with the close succession of the golden halos and the trumpets trespassing the limits of the frames. In the frieze below the three scenes half figures of Saints are inserted, identifiable by their attributes: *Lucia, Marta and margherita* below the *Wedding, Colomba, Maria Maddalena and Cecilia* below the *Presentation, Agnese, Agata and Orsola* below the *Annunciation.* Along the lower part of the arch six *tondi* enclose the *cardinal Virtues,* together with *Constance* and *Humility,* painted as a monocrome. The cycle of San Leonardo al Lago is unanimously attributed by critics to Lippi Vanni, one of the most representative artists in the Sienese figurative culture of the second half of the XIV century, sensitive ehir of the gothic tradition abruptly interrupted by Black Death in 1348. Another relevant painting is the fresco of the *Crucifixion,* occupying the whole length, more than four metres, of the left wall of what used to be the chapter house of the monastery, divided in 1810 by a screen which greatly damaged the large scene. Recognized by Berenson as a

work by the young Giovanni di Paolo, it has captured the attention of the scholars in the last few decades. It can be dated to 1445, and it expresses, with sharp, dramatic conciseness, the most recognizable features of the Sienese painter: the broken rhythm of the groups contrasting with the pained hieratic face of the Christ, translated in an ex-

asperated linearism, accentuated in the contrast of the monochrome figures against a red backgorund. An original historical excursion can be added as a complement to the visit to the Eremo: a detour which, following the CAI signs of track 123, leads to the Pyramid celebrating the XVIII century reclamation of the lake: under which begins the excellently preserved underground draining canal. Crossing it is quite a fascinating experience: on the walls, as it is docu-

mented in a recent reconnoissance by the Regione Toscana "one can notice several charcoal graffiti, drawings and calculations, dates, a saying, sketches of birds, human figures, sketches of how the stone-masons should cut the interlocking stones and the headstones". Although the visit does not present particular difficulties, it is anyway advisable to be accompanied by experts. For that matter, contact Ermanno Vigni (tel. 0577-221574) the Coordinator of the Committee for the Public Safeguard of Pian del Lago (Comitato per la Salvaguardia Pubblica di Pian del Lago), to whom must go the credit for having "rediscovered" and promoted the restoration and increase in value of the canal. During the Second World War, the passage was used as subterrenean depot for a military airport, obtained for the occasion from the old *polje*.

From the Eremo, we go back down to the junction, were we continue to the left meeting shortly afterdwards another junction with a tarmac road, to the right. After less than half a kilometre on this new road, we turn to the left, following the sign to Santa Colomba. The road climbs: on the left is the large block of Montebuono, in which, underneath the more recent, rustic layer, the traits of the medieval fortification are not difficult to detect. Especially regarding the various arched openings and architraves with convex corbels.
At the peak of the climb the small settlement of Santa Colomba is dominated, to the right, by the imposing

Villa Petrucci

83

The villa was built by Pandolfo Petrucci, Lord of Siena, between the end of the XV century and the beginning of the XVI, on the site of a medieval fortification, the traces of which are evident in the scarp. These were the remains of a fortified habitation once belonging to the Accarigi family, the tower of which was later transformed into the church bell tower. The building was seriously damaged during the raids of the troops lead by Giovanni Acuto (John Hawkwood), in 1364. The transformation into a villa took place with the passage of the ownership to Pnadolfo Petrucci, who took care of the remodelling which was perhaps designed by Baldassarre Peruzzi. The restoration was concluded in 1511. A further damage was caused by the passage of imperial troops during the War of Siena, in 1554: the villa was then newly restored by Alessandro Petrucci, bishop of Massa Marittima and Populonia, at the beginning of the XVII century. After his death (1629) the heirs handed it over to the Grand Duke Cosimo III, and then to the Collegio Tolomei, who turned it into a holiday home for the young Sienese noblemen in the XVIII century. Today, after various vicissitudes, it is private

property. The importance of the building is proved by a drawing of Giorgio Vasari the younger, preserved at the Gabientto Disegni of the Uffizi in Florence, depicting the state of the villa at the beginning of the XVII century: the plan highlights the helicoidal staircase, and a note in the lower margin signals the presence of a "very large and wonderful garden", on the back of the building, and of a lawn on the front. More architectural elements were added in the course of the centuries to the initial plan by Peruzzi. Two XVIII century lateral wings enlarged the palace, reducing the space of the garden; the upper storey was added, and the *limonaia*, in the XIX century. According to a legend, a long underground gallery, described by Merlotti, linked the villa with the so-called Palace of the Magnifico in Siena: "Admirable is the subterrenean passage existing as a prosecution of the more modern, magnificent and renowned spiral staircase, on an idea by Baldassarre Peruzzi, by which one descends 181 steps below the ground, and then continues along that murky hole for a long stretch, not able to find the destination as the soil on top is in various points falling down, as it is cretaceous and lacking in solidity; but all the rest is dug in stone, and they say it communicates with the other Palace in Siena, formerly of the Magnificent Pandolfo Petrucci, nearby the Pieve of San Giovanni".

On the left of the villa, on the other side of the road, is

la Parrocchiale (Parish Church)

dedicated to the saints Peter and Paul. According to a legend, it should be traced back to the will of a married couple, Giacomo di Martinuccio e Colomba di Taddeo, who allegedly had it erected in the XI century as a small oratory dedicated to the saints Giacomo (James) and Colomba, from their names. More probably, its origin is linked to the Ardengheschi, who owned vast portions of land in the area. The name of the parish church appears already in a 1105 document. In 1364 the building was devastated by Giovanni Acuto's troops. In 1486 it was made a *pieve*, parish church. The interior of the church was renovated in 1687: on that occasion, the XIV century fresco which embellished its walls were covered with a layer of white paint. Following the legacy of the parish priest Emilio Scarpellini, remodelling of the church started in 1709: first four side altars were built, and then the high altar, with

During the War of Siena, Santa Colomba was the scene of harsh battles against the imperial troops, related with liveliness by the chronicler Alessandro Sozzini, in date March 21 1554: the imperial troops "aimed their artillery at the fortress of Santa Colomba, where many peasants and women were, and no soldiers, who had previously brough many things and food supplies. The enemies sent their drummer to ask whether they wanted to come to terms; their answer was no; and immediately they started fighting it, and the stones killed some of those countrymen, and all the women started to cry: so much so that they surrendered unconditionally; once the enemies entered, they made all of them their prisoners, except the priest of that village (ser Girolamo of Bartolomeo Balsi), who retreated armed into the church, and never wanted to surrender, and died valiantly and there was no mercy for him. Having made all the men prisoners, they sent out the women and chose the peasants according to their liking, and they hanged 22 of them by the throat: which frightened all the neighbours; so much so that no one waited for them in the rest of the fortresses, everyone marched out of them and left them empty."

rich white stucco works in the baroque style.

The structures were destroyed in the intervention carried out in the Fifties, when the aim was to get back to the surface the "original" aspect of the church. On that occasion, the façade was altered, as well: the two round windows above the portal were closed and substituted by just one central round eye. Today the interior has a bare appearance, with a modern stone table. On the left, beside the entrance, is a XV century *Crucifix*; on he right, the photographic copy of the canvas depicting the *Virgin with Child in glory and the Saints Giacomo and COlomba*, once placed above the first altar on the left (the original is preserved in the Bishop's Palace in Siena). The frescoes on the back wall, behind the high altar, wihch were covered by a layer of paint, are now being restored thanks to the sponsorship of the Bank of Monteriggioni. The careful and delicate operation to recuperate the paintings is restoring the readability to the two large scenes, depicting the *Nativity* (on the left) and the *Curcifixion* (on the right), up to now dimmed by a thick white layer. The paintings can be dated back to the beginning of the XIV century for the marked

dependence on Duccio di Buoninsegna's manner. In the *Nativity* XIII century iconographic elements are still present, such as the cave sheltering the Virgin and the group of the wet-nurses. The unknown author, recently identified as the so-called "Master of the Buonconvento Cross", displays a strong bond with the Duccio's gothic lesson, in the dramatic intensity permeating the scene of the *Crucifixion*, and in the elegant flowing lines with which the body of the Christ and the garments of the sorrowful Saint John. On the right wall are more traces of the XIV century decoration, with a theory of four saints within arches, recognizable as Saint Ansano, Saint Bartholomew, a Bishop Saint and Saint Lawrence, the work of a painter active in the second half of the century. More fragmented are the remains on the apse wall, in the scarce rests of the scene represeting *Saint Nicholas saving two children* (first half of the XIV century) and *Cristo in pietà*, slighlty later. The Chapel of the *Compagnia della Madonna dei Sette Dolory* (Confraternity of the Virgin of the Seven Sorrows), founded in 1599 (under the name of Visitazione di Maria, changed a few years later), is reached through a small door beside the back wall. The high altar, erected in 1623, is surmounted by a gable with two little angels in white stucco, and contains the canvas depicting the *Virgin with Child and the Saints Pietro and COlomba*, commissioned by the brothers of the Confraternity in 1637 (according to Merlotti, to the Florentine painter Agostino Ciampelli). In the left corner at the bottom are the names of the patrons and the date the painting was executed: TADDEO FIORENTINO/ NICCOLO BARDI PRIORI/ 1637. At the sides are the frescoed *Saint Thomas and Saint Anthony Abbot*, bearing below the inscription with the names of the brothers who commissioned the work: Tommaso Massi e Antonio Bernardini. Both the paintings can be attributed to a Sienese painter of the beginning of the XVII century.

At the back of the villa, and at the end of the village, we advise to proceed along the gravel road. This route offers a supplement to the visit, consisting in a succession of small settlements maintaining interesting archaic features: Il Giardino, il Colle, Gavina, Casa Bocci. Just above il Colle, aat Cennano, particularly remarkable are the re-

mains of the walls of what used to be the *comune* of a XII century village in the Sienes countryside.
We then get back to Santa Colomba, from which we descend again on the Pian del Lago road and follow it to the left. After less than 1 km we turn left again, to visit the country hamlet of

Fungaia

"Some Sienese magnats had their lordship on Fungaia: Baldovino di Gherardino, who in October 1128, being in Siena, donated to the abbey of San Salvatore all"Isola the lands he owned in Lecore, and at Fungaia".

The origins of the church of San Michele Arcangelo probably date back to the XII century. The church was regulated under the law patronage of the parish church of Marmoraia until 1404, and then passed under San Lorenzo a Colle Ciupi; finally, after harsh disputes between the parish priests of the two churches, under Marmoraia again. It

never enjoyed considerable revenus, so little so that towards the end of the XV century it was annexed to the church of Santo Spirito in Siena. It was made autonomous again after a few years, and in 1520 it was endowed with some lots of land by the noble families of the Banchi and the Petrucci: nevertheless, it was united to San Lorenzo al Colle in 1592. In 1638 the church was enlarged and the rectory restored, to satisfy the needs of an increased population: the coats of arms of the Tancredi, Orlandini and Bichi families, who gave their financial contribution, remain from that intervention. According to tradition, a XVIII century copy of the large panel painted by Beccafumi for the Chiesa del Carmine, representing *The fall of the rebel angels*, had been placed on the high altar. The most recent restoration dates back to 1869, when the building was enlarged further towards the entrance, adding the orchestra, and the façade was rebuilt in bricks, and ornated by the new portal with a window above it. The only trace of the medieval period is inside: a small fresco on the right wall, representing *The Virgin with Child*, in bad condition, datable to the half XIV century and near to Niccolò di Segna's style. The walls are plastered and decorated on the bottom by a trompe-l'oeil marble border. The high altar goes back to the XVII century remodelling (1638), while the two side altars, dedicated to the Madonna del Buon Consiglio (Virgin of Good Advice) and to Saint Jospeh, were built in the XIX century.

Back on the Pian del Lago road, we proceed towards the left coasting the area which during World War II was used as an airport. We bypass the junction with the road to the Eremo, on the right, and after 300 metres we turn to the left closing at the Ceppo the ring of our route. A few metres before entering the Cassia, we turn to the left, for a last, fascinating detour towards a series of several, remarkable appointments with Sienese art.
The first is made of a compact system of medieval fortifications, articulated in an ideal quadrangle which, besides the dominating element, the Castello della Chiocciola, includes the settlemnets of La Villa, Casa Bucci and Castagnoli.

On the left, 500 metres from the road, is

La Villa

a large square tower, with a scarp interrupted on the south-east side by small doors with architraves and round arched windows, inserted in a square enclosure of walls with battlements. The windows on the upper storey have architraves on concave corbels; on top is the conclusive architrave, battled and slighlty protruding. Inside are frescoed decorations of remarkable interest, executed between the end of the XII century and the beginning of the XIV: geometrical patterns with diamonds and

quadrilobes, alternating with trompe-l'oeil curtains sustained by rings. Inside the enclosure, on the south-west side, an original buildings leans on the walls, with a portal and windows repeating those od the tower; the buildings on the other sides are later.

We now go back to the junction, where we turn left. After a short while we take a right, reaching in about half a kilometre

Castagnòli

It is a building of medieval origins, on a square plan, dating back to the XIII century: of this, the ogive windows are a proof. The façade was rebuilt in the XVI century, with two registers of porticos one above the other (later filled). It is plastered and dvided by brick cornices, sustaining round arches. A brick arch links the private chapel to the villa.

We trace our steps back to the same junction , on which

Casa Bucci

faces. It is a block of various buildings, some of them badly ruined, of evident medieval origin, as portals, doors and arched windows show. The remains of an ancient cloister and of a large well, probably destined to serve a religious community, are also visible. According to tradition, the original church of San Bartolomeo was built, the title of which was later transferred to Riciano.

Opposite Casa Bucci, on the other side of the road, is the

Chiocciola

The origins of the block date back to the XIV century, when the castle was built: in the XIX century the villa was built, leaning onto it, preceded by a three-arched portico. The oldest building leans on a scarp and features two towers on a rectangular plan, and a peculiar cilindric tower inside which is the stone spiral staricase, givng the name "chiocciola" (scala a chiocciola = spiral staircase) to the whole. the heigth of its steps is gradually reduced towards the top to give relief to those climbing up. The battlments of the towers dates back to last century's remodelling, when the Gothick addition substitued the original hammerbeam roof (still visible in the drawing Romagnoli made at the beginning of last century). The donjon "terminates with a raising jutting out in comparison to the lower storeys... masterly sustained by a series of brick arches unloading their own weight onto stone corbels." It used to be the property of the Turchi family (the same who built the so-called Palazzo Diavoli in Siena, also featuring a cylindric tower), the theatre of fights during the War of Siena, in strenuous defence against an army of more than a thousand Austrian and Spanish knights. Sozzini's chronicle thus relates the events: "On March 21 (1554) 1000 soldiers, and 100 knights of the enemies left, and headed off towards the Montagnola: once they arrived to a fortress called La Chiocciola, inside which several gentlemen were (that is to say Tommaso Turchi with three of his children, Antonio Turchi with two children and many peasants) as soon as they arrived they started fighting; because of which thing those inside gave their unconditional surrender, and were all made prisoners, setting free only the women and children". In the XVIII century the castle passed in the hands of the Brancadori, and was then won at cards by the Englishman O'Brien. Beside the main blocks are the agricultural buildings, the cellars and the chapel. Inside the villa, in the area of the private residence, is a cave where at the beginning of the century the owner, O'Brien discovered a series of prehistorical finds today preserved in the British Museum in London.

After the visit to the Chiocciola we continue on the gravel road climbing up and entering the woods. On the right, after 1 km, we meet the church of

San Bartolomeo a Riciano

surrounded by a wall. It was probably trasferred from Casa Bucci to here, where an oratory already was, at the beginning of the XIV century, when the parish priest started living here on a more permanent basis. It is one of the oldest churche sin the Monteriggioni territory, very much altered in the course of time. The façade, in big stone blocks, is preceded by a paved area; the one-nave building is today surrounded by private buildings. The presbitery is preceded by a stuccoed arch. In the XVIII century, the building was enlarged and embellished by three new altars: on the piers of the high altar is the coat of arms of the Brancadori family, the former owners of the Chiocciola, who had it built in 1713 and who commissioned the canvas representing *The Martyrdom of Saint Bartholomew*, a copy of the painting by Alessandro Casolani in the Chiesa del Carmine in Siena. The side altars were erected in 1740 by the Congregation of the Sacrament (the one on the right) and by the Palmieri family (the one on the left).

We continue going up, as on the right the green profile of the Montagnola makes itelf more and more evident, until we reach

Colle Ciupi

a village already mentioned in the first half of the XIII century. This area probably became so deserted after the damages caused by the 1555 war, so much so that in the XIX century Merlotti saw it as "an isolated and wild place". Nowadays, a careful action of restoration of the old stone houses has partly repopulated of "sunday inhabitants" this fascinating place.

The church, dedicated to San Lorenzo, is already mentioned in 1178 document, and in the XIV century it was bequeathed to the canons of the Duomo of Siena. Inspite of the modesty of its revenues, the parish church managed to furnish the building with a complete cycle of paintings of remarkable quality and artistic importance, starting from the end of the XIII century. The simple structure of the church has remained more or less untouched, without undergoing any significant transformation in the course of the centuries. In the façade is the portal with lunettes (maybe originally frescoed), and on the top a small round window; on the right side is the portal leading into the cloister. There are two mullioned windows on the north side and on the back wall. The vaulted bell tower seems to date back to the same period as the church. A recent intervention of analysis and research on the internal surfaces of the little church of Colle Ciupi has revealed most of the

rich and moving pictorial cycle ornating the building from the beginning of the XIV century. The frescoes being brought back to the surface by a careful restoring campaign can be dated back to that period, thus adding a new and fundamental contribution to the knowledge of the art of wall painting which developed around Duccio di Buoninsegna. The master's panel painting style is well known, but his activity in the filed of frescoed paintings must still be explored. In the last century, feeble traces of those paintings had already appeared, coming to light, although quite faint, underneath the XVIII century layer, when, using the outraged words of the parish priest Merlotti "a barbarous hand covered them in white paint, when, once decayed the spirit of beautiful things, artistic works were not appreciated any monger, and the doing of whitewashers is proposed to the immortal works of the most valiant artists". The cycle is composed of sophisticated and intense scenes, sustained by the liveliness of colours, testifying the relevance the place must have in the Middle Ages. Inside, frescoes cover up all the walls of the building: their peculiarity lies in the repetition, at the distance of a few decades, of the same subject: the *Madonna enthroned with Child and Saints*, the so-called *Maestà*, as a confirmation of the intense devotion for the cult of the Virgin in that place. The oldest painting is the one behind the altar, where in the triangle of the tympanum is the Christ in the almond, and a flying angel, and below, beside the small window, is the *Maestà*: similarly, on the left wall is again a *Maestà with Saint Peter*, at the sides *St John the Evangelist* (on the left) and *St Paul* (on the right). The *Maestà* on the right wall is preceded, to the left, by *Stories of St Catharine*, by the whole figure of *St Catherine*, while on the right side it is delimitated by the figure of *St Paul*. The stylistic features of the cycle are still being studied and researched: at least two artistic personalities can be distinguished, acting in the orbit of Duccio di Buoninsegna, which confirms the liveliness and variety of enterprises undertaken by the master's workshop in the Sienese artistic world at the beginning of the XIV century.

At Colle Ciupi, the gravel road terminates: here begins a medieval route (corresponding to the CAI track n. 102) on which it is worth the while taking a at least a short stroll.

137

No tarmac nor engines

"Sometimes I doubt whether motorists know what grass is, or what flowers look like, because they never looked at them while passing by slowly. If you show a motorist a greenish spot, Oh Yes, *he will say,* that's grass! *If you show him a pink patch, he will say it is a rose-bush, while the houses to him are white spots and the brown ones, cows grazing".* These are Ray Bradbury's words, in a famous eulogy of *slow foot*: a cognitive modality and, at the same time, almost a literary genre. Also practiced, among many others, by Cesare Pavese: *"I did not envy cars. I knew that by car you cross a land, you do not get to know it.* On foot *I would have told Pieretto,* go to the true countryside, you take the paths, you walk along the vineyards, you see everything. It is as different as looking at the water or jumping into it."

Such *auctoritas* is a comfort, but after all, nowadays we might even leave it aside. Putting reasonable limits to the indiscriminate use of motor vehicles is today part of common sense: and we all know that driving a carr does not mean choosing an absolute condition of being and travelling. Very pragmatically, using the car is convenient for those moves to which we do not entrust any special cognitive investment: literally considering it a "means". A means

we conveniently get out of, once we arrive at the threshold of the space we are most interested in getting close to: opening the trunk and taking rucksack and trekking boots out of it; taking off the roof our mountain byke; or getting on a horse or even on a hot-air baloon. In any case, continuing our journey in a different and more pleasant way.

On foot

We are not wayfarers any longer, either in our daily habits or in the meaning proposed by dictionaries: "those who cover a long distance on foot".
Foot as a means of transport luckily are not a need these days, but an option: to be carried out in our spare time, as the increasing popularity of trekking confirms, also in terms of marketing: a recent word denominating an old experience, and a particularly relevant one to the territory of Monteriggioni. This is an area which was "born" and which developed culturally precisely as a crossroads of pedestrian routes: from the prehistoric ones to the "francigeni" (i.e. coming from France).
However, we are no longer pilgrims or migrants, either. Walking along the traces of old routes is a similar process to that of proposing again medieval food and the inevitable mediations linked to it, between a faithful reconstruction and the actual possibility to put it into effect. However, everything is permitted when one plays games with imagination: an activity which, in Monteriggioni, is legitimated and almost provoked by its extraordinary peculiarity. That is to say, the existence of long stretches of medieval paving, perfectly preserved. In fact, there are a few more areas in Tuscany where remainders of historic road systems come to the surface. But they always cover short or very short distances: like erudite quotations surviving in irreversibly altered itineraries and enviroments. On the other hand, here, and especially between Monteacuto and Montemaggio, entire routes feature the continuity of an age-old paving: an *unicum*, the importance and protection of which should be put on the same plan as the rest of the historical remains in the territory.
While searching "the way it was", pedestrian practice offers further elements of concreteness. Most of all, concerning the possibility to experiment old routes: "sewing

up", according to the original road logic, places which, on the contrary, appear as unconnected if visited using the modern raod network. Thus, enlightening connections are reconstructed, which would otherwise be dimmed by the hurried and absolute equation between engines and routes. The heart of the Montagnola, unreachable by car, does not correspond to an impossibility of itineraries and links, which on the contrary appear to be numerous and interlocked while walking.

Furthermore, walking allows us to recuperate more advisable sensations, tied to the seduction of the anthropological universe rather than to the sophisticated punctuality of the historic restoration: such as the emotion to get near a pass, the visual pleasure of a ridge, the track following the natural morphology of the terrain, all the clues that make us perceive the proximity of a house or a village.

Knowkedges and sensations such as these present themselves as well-organized and easy to experiment in this area, thanks to two converging enterprises, carried out by CAI (Club Alpino Italiano) and by the Province of Siena.

The Sienese section "Umberto Vivi" of the CAI has worked both on maps and on location. The classic white and red symbols (on stones, tree trunks, walls, corners) mark a thick network of tracks, covering the whole area of the Montagnola, and organized according to numbered routes. A map has also been published: on the recto the routes are highlighted in red, while on the back their detailed description also includes historical and naturalistic information. These are the routes covering the Monteriggioni territory.

101 - From Abbadia a Isola to the Cassia

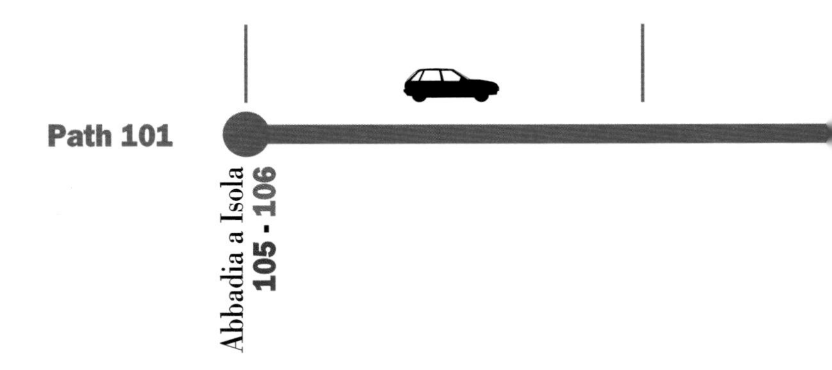

8 km, 160 metres ascent and 65 descent, in about 2 hours. From Abbadia follow the asphalt road to Monteriggioni, then detour after about 200 metres on a flat gravel road which, after 1,5 km, climbs up into the woods where, in an opening are the excavations of the Etruscan site of Campassini (the name of the countyhouse below). Further on,

171

102 - From Monteriggioni to Santa Colomb

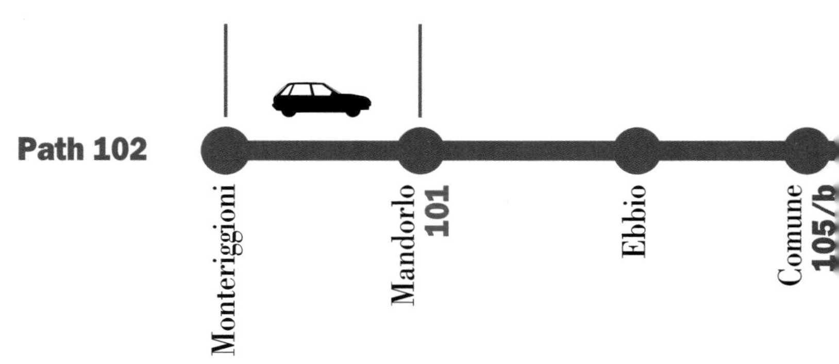

14 km, 340 metres ascent and 300 descent in about 4 hours.
Leave Monteriggioni by the Porta Franca, and descend along the asphalt until the Cassia. Cross the Cassia and then continue along the gravel road leading to Case Mandorlo (crossing route 101) and then to Ebbio. Continue on a steep hill until Casa Comune, after having just met route

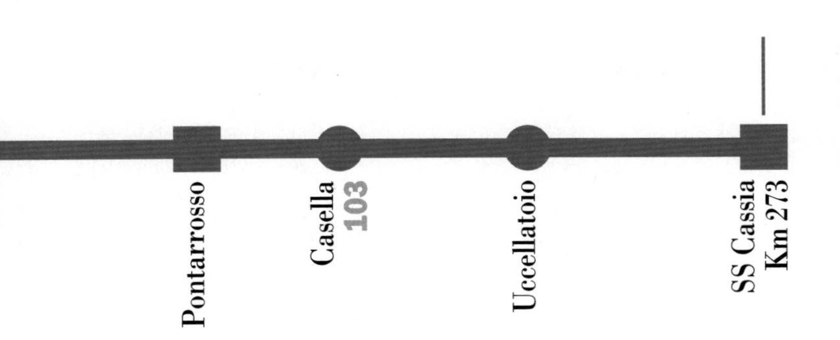

bypass Case Mandorlo (where an inn was in the XVII and XVIII century)and then cross Route 102: after having crossed a stream, thanks to the old bridge of Pontarrosso, continue bypassing Casella (crossing route 103). The Cassia is reached along the gravel road leading to the Uccellatoio.

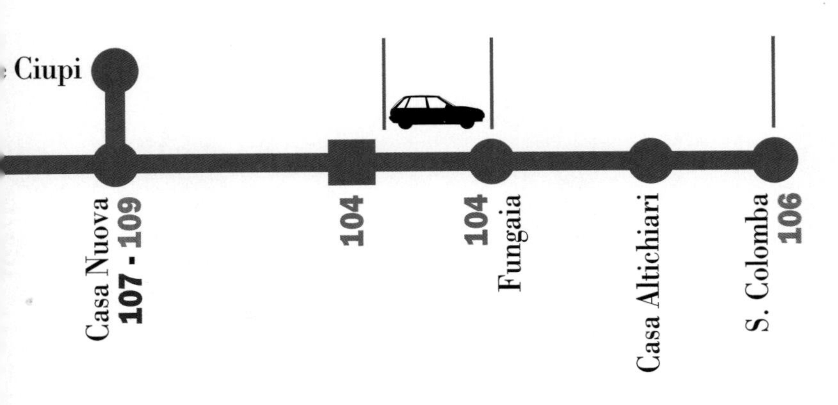

105 B, which is followed for about 500 metres, then detouring to the right and reaching Colle Ciupi. Here, overlap route 107 for a short stretch and then go straight on until the hamlet of Fungaia. Continue on the right leaving the strada comunale in favour of a path which touches Casa Altichiari and reaches Santa Colomba.

103 - From the Cassia to Pian del Lago

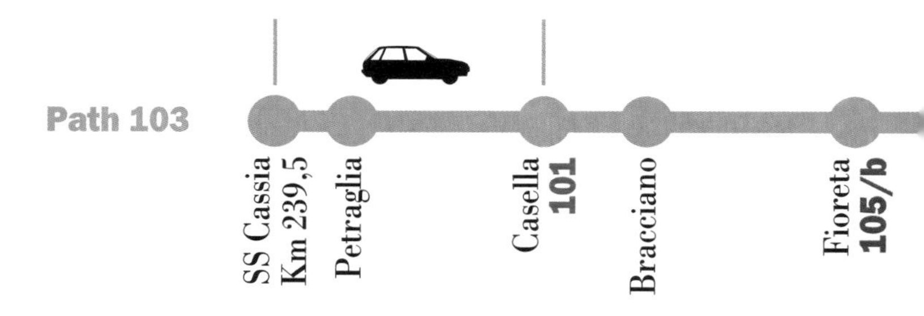

On the Cassia, at km 239,5, Stomennano junction, take the gravel road passing by Petraia and Casella. Keeping on the border to cultivated fields, climb up until Casella, crossing, at 297 metres, route 101. Continue going up until Bracciano (348 mt.) and then, in the woods, Fioreta (556 mt. a beautiful medieval building formed by two blocks linked by a long stone wall, with arched portals: the big-

104 - From Fungaia to Scorgiano

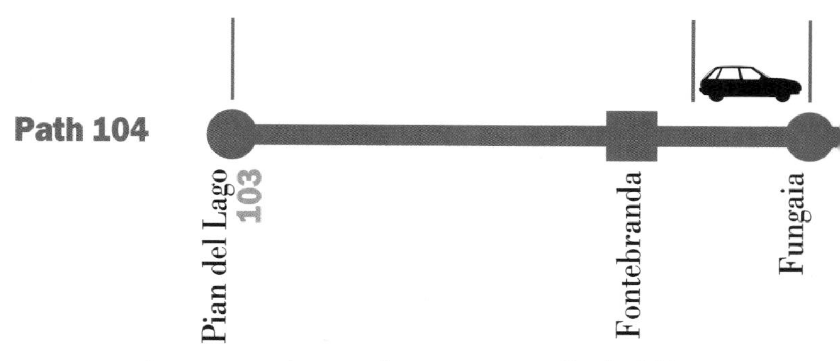

15 km, 350 metres ascent, 350 descent, 4 and a half hours. From the stud at Pian del Lago cross the field, which once was an airport, overlapping route 103, which is left on the right, after about 1,5 km, to continue in the woods and reach Fungaia after having passed the stream Fontebranda. Leave route 102 and continue to the right on a track going uphill, which, after about 1200 metres, crosses route 102 again. Further on, after crossing route 106, go over a river on an old bridge and arrive to Casa Alteri after about 1,5 km. Pass through a field and then descend into a forest on the right, reaching the Nagli Chapel. The building,

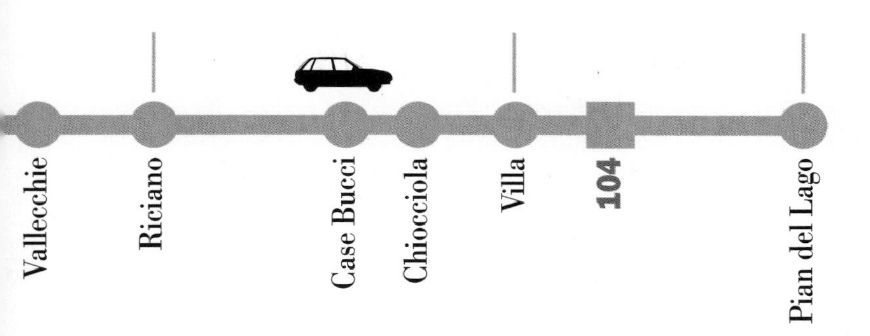

ger building has a tower in a corner, while the other one has an orignal opening and external staircase). Go down to Vallecchie, on the left, and then to Riciano: continue to the left on the road that, if you detour on the right at Case Bucci, lets you get to the Castello della Chiocciola and finally, passing through La Villa, reaches Pian del Lago.

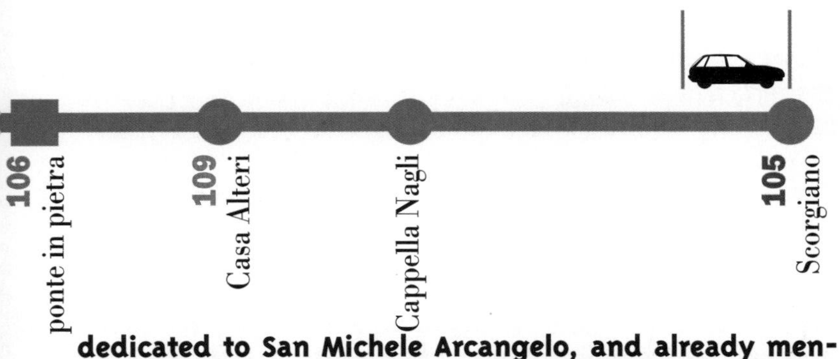

dedicated to San Michele Arcangelo, and already mentioned in a 1171 document, is today totally abandoned, hidden underneath thick bushes. The roof has fallen in, while the walls f the nave are still visible together with the charming remains of the semi-circular apse with a small window in the middle. The remains of the façade are whitewashed. In the XII century it belonged to the monks of Abbadia a Isola. Further on, cross route 106 and, after about 1 km, route 105, on which you continue to the left until you reach Scorgiano.

105 - From Abbadia a Isola to Scorgiano

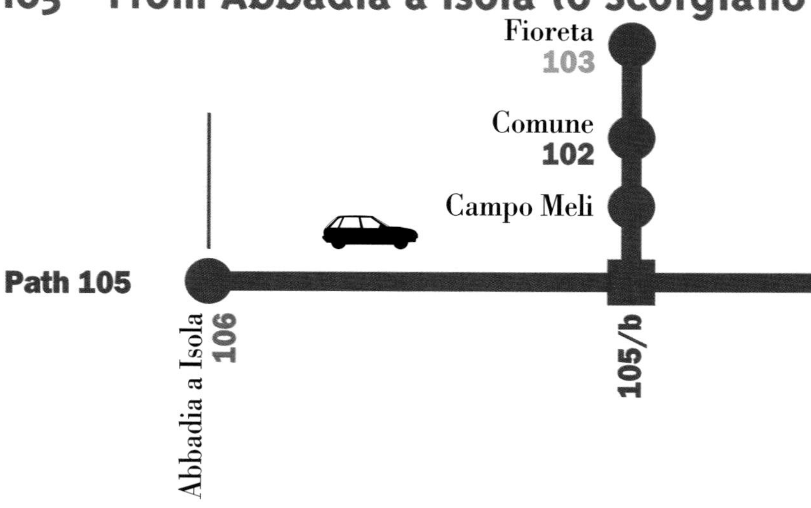

12 km, 390 metres ascent, 280 descent, 4 hours on the way out and 3 and a half on the way back.

73

From a cart-road starting just above Abbadia a Isola, go up and then turn right at the octagonal chapel. The route then continues in the woods, with beautiful views of Monteriggioni, meeting a monument to the partisans and, further on, route 105/b, coming from the right. After about 1,5 km, pass the stretch of route 106 leading to, on the left, Monte Maggio, and continue following the same numbering as the other stretch of 106, reaching Casa Giubileo (500 metres). Abandon route 106 and continue until Montauto. Here, in panoramic position, once was a castle belonging to the Lambardi: it was afterwards handed on, not without contrasts, to the monks of Abbadia a Isola and finally to the Soarzi. Its power grew during the course of the XII century, when the castle took over the near castle of Monte Maggio in controlling the territory. In Repetti, *ad vocem*: "Finally to this Montagutolo the name of "del Bosco" is added in a documento issued in that place on March 5 1528. It was the sale for a undred Sienese liras by a certain Grazia of the later Giovanni from Montagutolo del Bosco, to Bartolo of the later Tolomeo de' Tolomei from Siena, of a lot of land situated in a place called la Lama a Castornaja."

74

During the Aragonese war of 1478-1479 the castle was occupied by the Florentines who, unable to keep it, decided

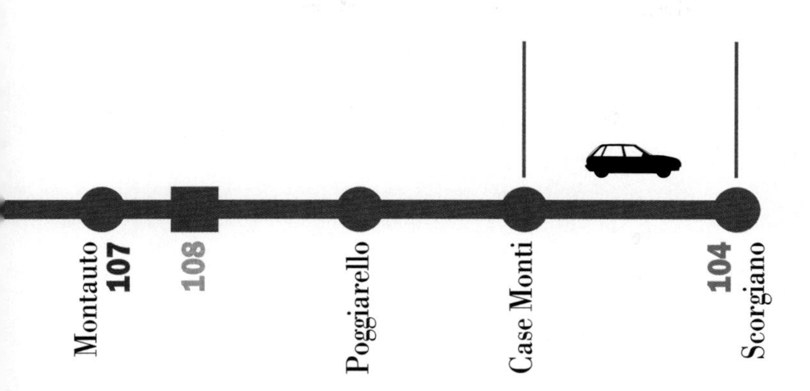

to "burn it and pull it down" together with Montecastelli. All that remains today are two small towers facing on to the valley and other fragments of walls, among which is a door with architrave and beautiful corbels, now part of a farmhouse, with a well and an oven. A few ruins is all that remains also of the church of San Biagio, on a rectangular plan and with a trussed roof, appearing in a XII century document listing twenty churches under the jurisdiction of Abbadia a Isola. Below, in the woods, are walls placed in concentric circles, possibly recognizable as the wreck of a prehistoric fortification.
Descend from Montauto on route 107, and then leave it on the left, following route 108 and then detouring off it, on the right, passing the houses of Poggiarello, Monti, and finally reaching Scorgiano.

105/b - From the Campo Meli junction to Fioreta

3,5 km, 80 metres ascent, 50 descent
From the monument to the partisans, leave route 105 continuing to go up towards Campo Meli and then Comune where, from Monteriggioni, also arrives route 102: continue for about 400 metres, leaving then route 102 to go on the right, descending onto Fioreta

106 - From Abbadia a Isola to S. Colomba

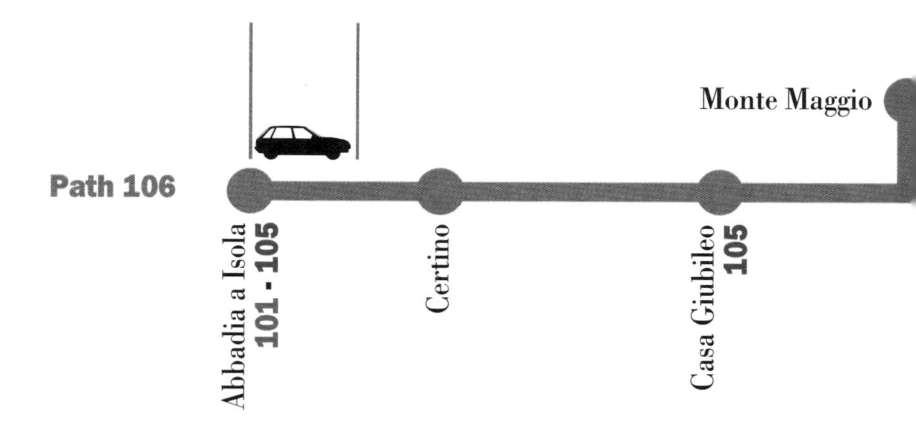

12 km, 460 metres ascent, 300 descent, 3 hours
From Abbadia a Isola, go up the gravel road arriving in two kilometres to Certino farmhouse, and then continue, still up the hill, until Casa Giubileo. The route is now the same as 105, from which you must detour again after 300 metres continuing on the right and meeting after about 1 km, on the left, a short detour to the top of monte Maggio (671 mt.). The main route goes towards the Castellare di Monte Maggio (658 mt.).
"In April 1247, Cammarosano writes, a representative of the Sienese Comune took formal possession of the 'forest and land of Monte Maggio, until the ancient castle called Castellare di Monte Maggio, in the place named Poggio di Vignale.': he performed symbolic acts of ownership, 'taking and breaking with his own hands wood and branches of the aforementioned forest, and taking, uprooting and picking up soil, grass and stones from the same place', and he forbade some locals to go and get wood in that stretch of forest". From the definition *old castle* we can infer that that fortification, once important for the control it could perform over the Via Francigena, was then in a state of decay, or ruined. The castle was mentioned in 1086-87 documents of Abbadia a Isola, together with its church, dedicated to Santa Maria. Its importance gradually diminished towards the half XII century and it ended up de-

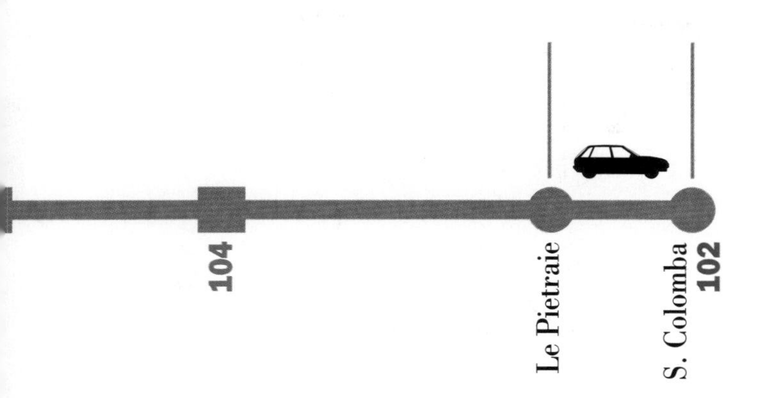

pending from Montauto, when the church, too, was transformed into a romitory: the destination of many pilgrimages from the countryside until not long ago. The only remainder of the wall structure is a beautiful round tower, surrounded by vegetation.
The route then overlaps route 109, whch is left at a junction continuing, on the left, on route 107: after 400 metres, take a path on the right. After a forest, a slight descent on a mule-track terminates at Le Petraie: from here go down the asphalt until Santa Colomba.

107 - From Castel Petraia to Colle Ciupi

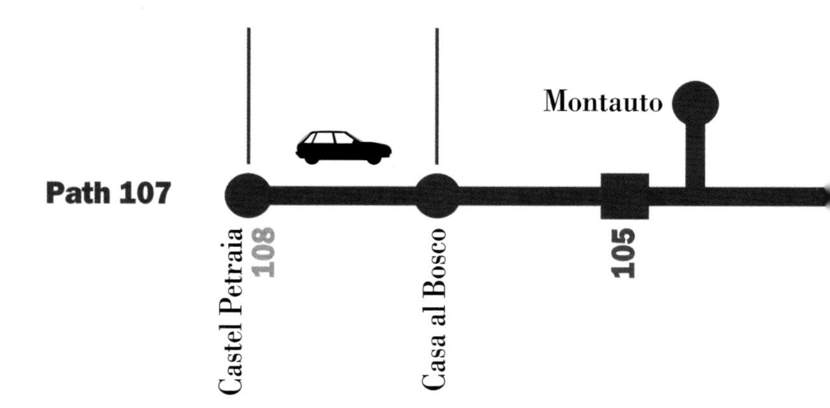

9,5 km, 300 metres ascent, 130 descent, 3 hours on the way out, 2 and a half on the way back.
From Castel Petraia, go up a large white road on the same route as 108 from which a detour on the right continues on a nice paved road overlapping route 105 and then leaving

108 - From Castel Petraia to Marmoraia

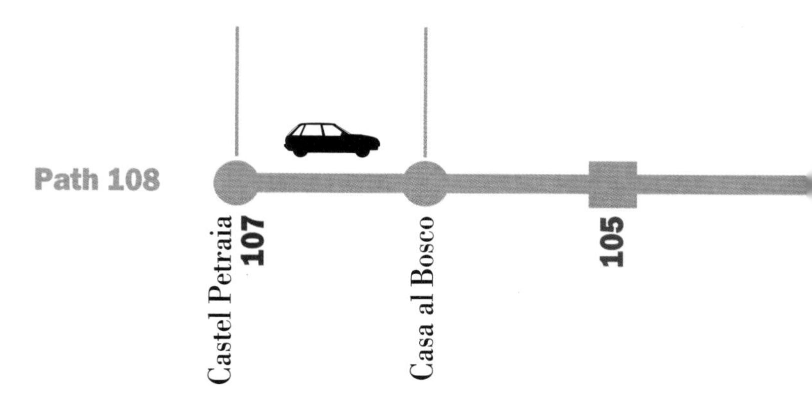

10 km, 360 metres ascent, 90 descent, 3 hours on the way out, 2 and a half on the way back.
From Castel Petraia go up a wide gravel road overlapping route 107, then leave it as it overlaps route 105. Continue until Casa Nagli: after about 1 km the route meets route 104, proceeding alongside with it for about 200 metres, and leaving it to descend on the left on a mule-track.

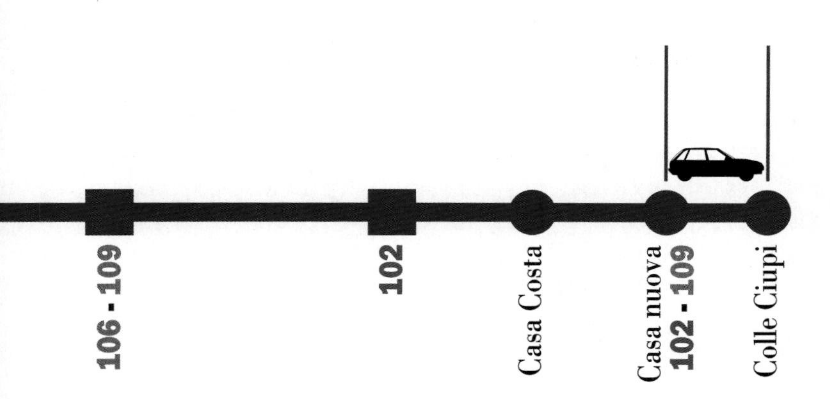

it at a junction (from which Montauto is within a short distance), thus continuing on the right. After 3 km, the route meets routes 106 and 109, and, further on, 102. On descending, Casa Costa is on the right. On a paved road, protected by two walls, the route gets to Colle Ciupi.

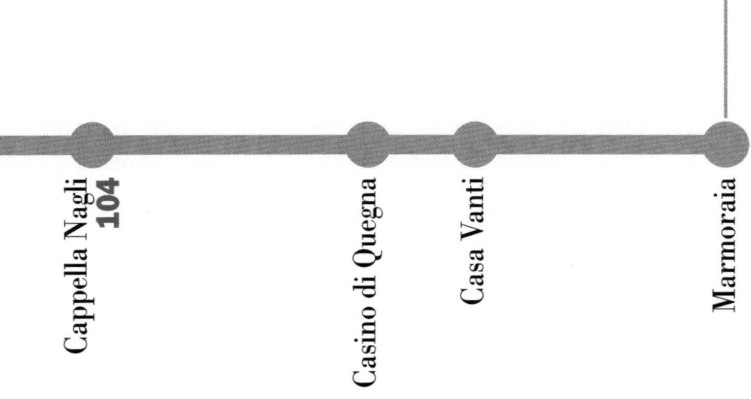

Climb up again, crossing a chestnuts teres grove, to Casino di Quegna, and then to the asphalted road linking Scorgiano to Celsa. Follow it for about 100 metres on the right, and then leave it at Casa Vanti where you take a mule-track going downhill into the woods. After meeting a spirng (with a tap), take a left at the next junction, on the track going up to Marmoraia.

The Province of Siena has inserted the Monteriggioni area, partly overlapping CAI's network of trekking routes, in a trekking network unique to this country: covering over 600 km, with 306 signposts insicating the routes, and also all the places of historical and artistic interest. Ideally, but above all in actual fact, Monteriggioni can then represent a starting point for a visit on foot of the entire territory of the province. This includes the important art centres alongside with the most secluded corners, in a forever surprising landscape.
There are seven main routes, linked with the network of Monte Amiata, of the province of Viterbo, Grosseto, the Chianti area and the Val di Chiana (Arezzo):

1. Monteriggioni - Gracciano d'Elsa - Casole d'Elsa - Monteguidi - Radicondoli - Podere Spagna - Terme della Galleraie - Chiusdino

2. Siena Taverne d'Arbia - Cuna - Radi - Murlo - La Befa - Montalcino - Abbazia di Sant'Antimo - Castelnuovo dell'Abate.

3. Trequanda - Sinalunga - Bettolle - Torrita di Siena - Montefollonico - Montepulciano - Chianciano - Sarteano-Chiusi - Cetona - San Casciano dei Bagni - Celle sul Rigo.

4. Monteriggioni - Strove - Marmoraia - Sovicille - San Rocco a Pilli - Bagnaia - Radi - Cuna - Torre a Castello - Asciano - Serre di Rapolano - Rapolano Terme- Belsedere - Trequanda.

5. Chiusdino - Monticiano - Bagni di Petriolo - Castiglion del Bosco - San Giovanni d'Asso- Abbazia di Monte Oliveto Maggiore - Belsedere - Trequanda.

6. Castelnuovo dell' Abate - Ripa d'Orcia - San Quirico d'Orcia - Pienza - Monticchiello - Montepulciano - Lago di Montepulciano.

7. Sovicille - Rosia - Pentolina - Monticiano.

On pedals

Mountain bykes are very popular these days. In the market exchange of television sales it enjoys the same ratings as TV sets and stereos. This recent mechanical device has known a rapid career, after having been conceived in the States, always insatiable as far as athletics go. At first, during the Tirthies, there was the old Schwinn "Excelsior", a heavy fat-tyred byke used to deliver newspapers: afterwards, in the Seventies, the ingenousness of people like Gary Fisher and Joe Breeze managed to transform it in a device able to face impossible climbs and breackneck descents. Its launch in Italy dates back to 1983, when "Airone" magazine proposed it christening it, puristically, "Rampichino" (little climber): from then on, the object itself gained momentum, if not the name. Experts do not even talk about mountain bykes alone, but they treatise over MTB (Mount Terrain Byke), ATB (All Terrain Byke) and CB (Country Byke).
A mountain byke can even get to Monteriggioni by train, at the station of Castellina Scalo, just below. A post-modern coupling recuperating and integrating at their best two different means of transport, rashly considered as surpassed in recent times of unsustainable developments. Moreover, it is possible to rent pountain bykes at the Euro Club di Rinaldi (via Cassia nord 33, Castellina Scalo, tel. 0577 305015, 305002), offering technical assistance and indications for every taste on the possible routes. One of these is offered as a "package", occupying an entire day: breakfast at the Monteriggioni castle, lunch in Trasqua forest, supper and relax at the Quornia lake, and then back by car. On request, other guided trips can be organized in collaboration with the Pro Loco of Monteriggioni. Otherwise Rinaldi, following the "do it yourself" mentality, puts at the disposal of anyone who is interested all the maps, detailed and easy to interpret, in order to let daytrippers sort out a wide range of options autonomously. The option called *campestre* starts among vineyards

and olive groves around the castle of Monteriggioni, reaches the route of an ancient cattle road, the "Maremmana", and terminates among the farmhouses and countryhouses of the Chianti. Most of the tracks on the Montagnola can be scoured on a mountain byke. The *Francigena,* of medium difficulty, starts from Abbadia Isola and reaches Siena along the traces of the omonymous medieval road, parallel with the Cassia and the Autopalio on some stretches. The *panoramica* option offers total relax, passing through easy Chianti roads. Also uneventful are the links with nearby famous art centres, from San Gimignano to Volterra.

On horseback

In June 1269, after the Florentine victory, a local chronicler tells how "the waters of the nearby Lago Chiaro and the swirling whirlpools of the Lago Scuro swallowed the flaming light of the communal standard together with the gallopping dispersed knights of the Sienese army." Today, not far from there, horses and riders turn round and round on the exercise track of the trainer Vittorio Taddei (after Abbadia a Isola, before the Casone, tel. 0577 305125 and 0336 472107) who, on request, organizes daytrips on the entire territory of Monteriggioni: particularly on the Montagnola. Taddei is also planning itineraries corssing the Appennines and the Alps, towards France and Spain, in a modern revisitation of the *aventure* and of the *quête* experienced and sought for by the "wandering knights" of the Arthurian and occitane tradition.
Pegasus Club (53035 Monteriggioni, Località il Fontino, 0577 304787 and 055 8073163) also offers excursions around Monteriggioni, besides providing boxes for horses, exercise tracks, etc.) and by the renowned Club Ippico at Pian del Lago.

Flying

As the Montgolfier brothers guessed and put into practice in 1783, it is possible to fly up high in the skies above in a wicker basket lifted off the ground by a ballon inflated with hot air: today this can still be experimented in the skies above Monteriggioni. The qualifying signs of the territory can thus be read by a fascinating angle, providing a different analysis: from the boundary walls to the slopes, from the farmhouses to the lakes of Sant'Antonio, from the colours of the woods to the network of roads and tracks. The venture is organized by the Baloon Club "Il Porto" (53010 Pianella - Siena), and the trips, for a maximum of 5 p., must be booked by telephone (0577/363232-363152): the perfect occasion to touch the top of the trees and raise up to 3000 feet above the ground. The journey through air obviously begins on the ground, with the spectacular operation of the inflating of the balloon, to which one can participate, helping the crew. Once off the ground, the wind will furnish the power, suggesting the best direction: each journey is different. On the other hand, the interpretation of the basket as an ideal platform for taking pictures and shooting films, remains a constant feature.

Landing is due in about one and a half hours, and tradition imposes a toast with champagne: a four-wheel drive especially equipped, which will have followed the flight, will provide the goods and take the participants back to the take-off point.

The flights are organized from april to september, also during the week: if the weather allows it, departure is due at dawn, to enjoy the sunrise at its best.

The Club wishes to point out that this experience does not require any specific skills: all the abilities you need are getting in and out of the basket, and stand up while you are in it. You shuold only wear comfortable shoes to walk in the fields: the Club will provide you with gloves and hats for the flight. It also worth speciying that balloon flights hold the world record as the safest amongst all the air sports. Pilots and crew can also boast a long standing experience, and the hot-air balloons they use are built by the best factory in the world, Cameron.

Abbadia a Isola-Montemaggio-Abbadia

The route follows a ring structure, on a gravel road on you which you can either walk, ride a mountain byke or drive, for a total length of 5 kilometres.
This route holds many memories dating back to the Liberation days. These woods were witnessees to the sacrifice of 17 young partisans, remembered by a monument erected on the spot of the execution. This episode is celebrated each year on the last Sunday in March, with a festival organized by the Comuni of the Mid-Val d'Elsa (Monteriggioni, Casole, Colle val d'Elsa, San Gimignano, Poggibonsi and Certaldo). Furthermore, the route is interesting for the observation and the knowledge of the landscapes and of the naturalistic side of the Monte Maggio. Along the way, it is possible to stop at Casa Giubileo, an old restored farmhouse, now functioning as a holiday home for young people, and as a laboratory for schools. Further excursion, either on foot or on a byke, can be made from Casa Giubileo to Castellare or Montauto.
The route begins a few metres above Abbadia a Isola, on a gravel road leaving the Strove road on the left. The identification of the road is made easier by the presence, on the right, of the signs of the Amministroazione Provinciale. After less than a hundred metres, we meet an octagonal chapel on the left; going on, we get to a crossroads dominated by a big oak-tree. The road on the left leads into the woods. After a few metres we meet an agricultural structure, with houses and garages for tractors; the road gets into the thick of the wood, coasting Monte Maggio. On both sides you can admire the typical vegetation of the Montagnola, in particular oak-trees and holm-oaks, closing the view on the Padule del Canneto, below, and towards the castle of Monteriggioni. Shortly afterwards, the road changes direction and points firmly to the top of the hill; the climb gets steeper. After some traces of old charcoal pits, on the left, a few metres within each other, two gravel roads leave the main road and soon join, linking, along a fascinating route, some farm houses ubicated on one side of Monte Maggio until Fioreta, descending afterwards and reaching the Cassia near Pian del Lago.
Continuing on the main road, after a short while we meet

the monument to the young partisans, eroded by time, and a stone with the names of the victims. Behind a small dry wall is an opening in the woods.

112

The road continues following a direction that makes a right angle with the sides of the mountain, and then bends to the west, as the climb becomes less steep. We coast the sides of the mountain, going up and down, until reaching a small opening from which the 106 CAI track to the Castellare departs. These are the places where old fortifications used to stand, giving birth to a popular legend noted down by Ciro Marzocchi in the last century: "the soldier woman".

The departure of these tracks is the highest point in the while circuit. From now on the road descends, and after less than a hundred metres Casa Giubileo pops out, in the middle of some openings, old traces of an abandoned agricultural activity.
Casa giubileo has been restored and furnished as a holiday home for summer stays, for the young and not so young. A large and modern kitchen, a dining room, a space for meetings functioning also as reading room and some rooms, bedding about twenty people, form the structure, to which are joined some rooms hosting a didactic laboratory for the study of history. The latter has been deviced as a photographic, sound and film archive, equipped with all the instruments (tape and video recorders, projector) and a specialized library on World War II and the history of the territory. Young people can use documentary material and make up dossiers with different forms of expression. From Casa Giubileo, the road rapidly descends onto the flatland below. In comparison with the previous route, this one is steeper. In some traits of the stretch on top, beyond the top of the trees the Chianti hills or the nearest houses of Colle val d'Elsa can be sighted. The direction often makes a right angle with the side of the mountain, and the descent is often interrupted by sharp bends. The forest terminates suddenly, giving way to cultivated areas. They are the fields and the houses of Certino, a small settlement of houses at the borders of the forest. The narrow road proceeds along a wall formed by large stones. Beyond it are some olive groves, further on accompanied by vine-

yards. The ferrous soil appears, as it did at the Chiocciola and in other parts of Monte Maggio, of a lively red colour: the typical "terra di Siena". The absence of the forest allows a view of the flatland below, the northermost part of the Monteriggioni territory: the Casone plain. Near a high cypress tree is the first crossroads. On the left, after a few metres we reach the road that takes from Abbadia to Strove, the Traversa dei Monti. Shortly afterwards we reach the end of te circuit, at Abbadia, where the route began.

The Via Francigena

The historian Sestan used a happy and lapidary definition for the medieval origin and development of Siena, calling the city "the daughter of the road", to underline the importance of its ubication regarding the road network of that time. Particularly, its position was central in relation to the different routes of the Francigena/Romea Road, linking Rome with central and northern Europe, and with Santiago de Compostela.

175

Historical reasons (the fall of the Roman empire) and changes in the conditions of the soil (many valley bottoms turning into swamps) had contributed to modify, in the early Middle Ages, the road network in central Italy. In the VII and VIII centuries, fights between the Longobards and the Byzantines for the control over Italy, and the need of the formers to find a safe route linking their capital, Pavia, with Lucca and the other capitals of the central and southern duchies (Spoleto and Benevento), made them choose a new itinerary for the crossing of Tuscany, safer both than the Aurelia, on the Tirreno coast, and the Cassia, which crossed the Val di Chiana.

The new route, coming from northern Italy, after having crossed the Appennines at the Cisa pass, touched Lucca, important Longobard city, crossed the river Arno and went up the left side of the hills of the Val d'Elsa, passing through San Genesio, Gambassi and San Gimignano. From here it started descending, wading the river Elsa near Gracciano, where it had a limited flow being in the proximity of the spring. Once entered in the present territory of Monteriggioni, the Francigena road lapped the slopes of the Monte Maggio touching Borgo Nuovo (where Abbadia a Isola would later be founded) and reaching Siena. From here, crossing the Val d'Arbia first, and then the Val d'Orcia and the Val di Paglia, the road reached Bolsena joining the old route to Rome.

59

The victory of Charle Magne, king of the Francs, over the Longobard king Desiderio, lessened the military importance of the new route, which became a stretch of the more complex road, the Via Francigena, which linked the central and northern regions with Rome.

Rome and the Holy Sepulchre in Jerusalem became the destinations of a flow of pilgrims. Even when, at the end of the XII century, the Holy Places fell into the hands of the Turks, the continuous pilgrimage did not stop. On the contrary, the Jubilee of the year 1300, announced by pope Bonifacius VIII, gave new

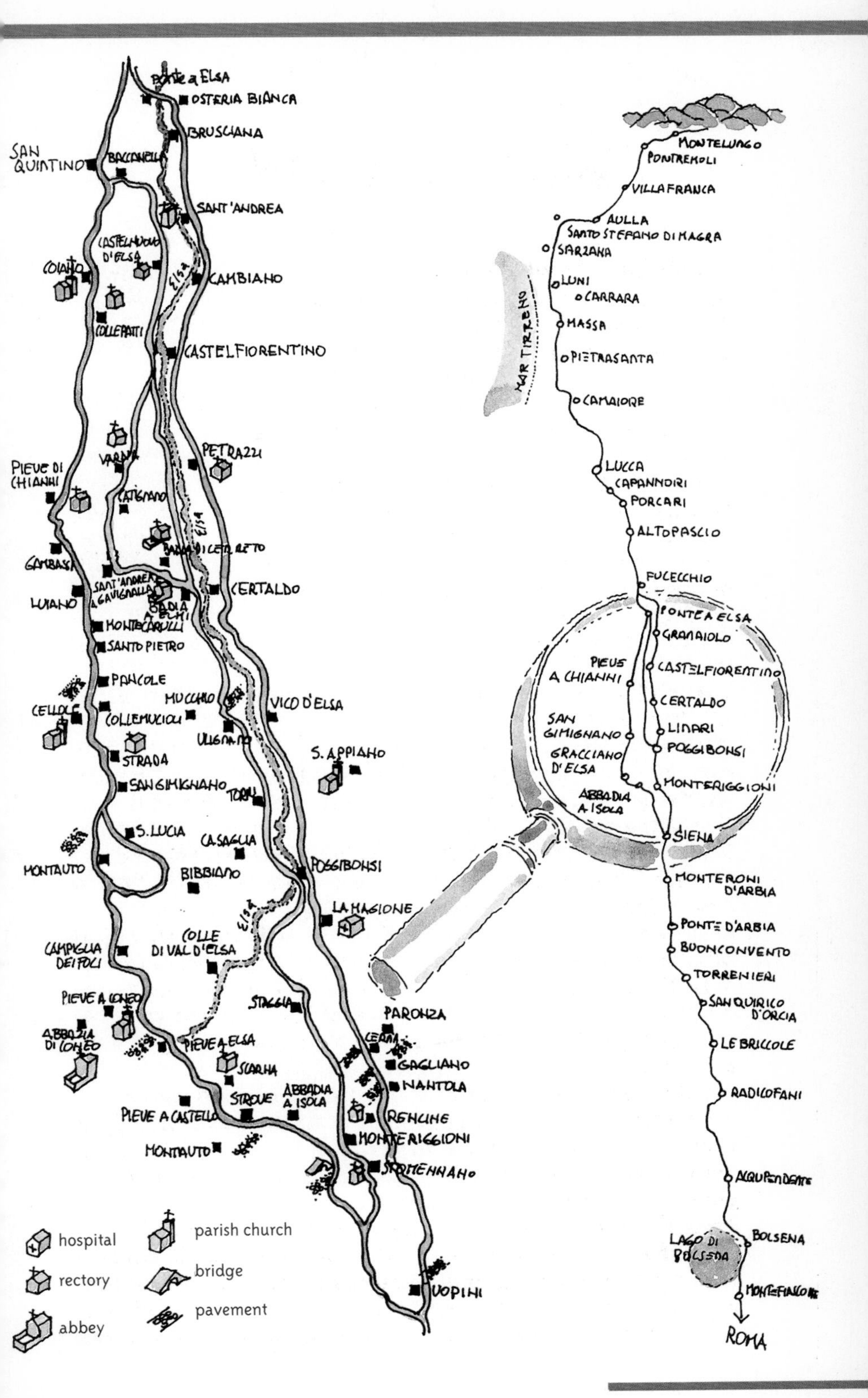
Ponte a Elsa
OSTERIA BIANCA
BRUSCIANA
SAN QUINTINO
BACCANELLA
SANT'ANDREA
CASTELNUOVO D'ELSA
COIANO
CAMBIANO
ELSA
COLLEPATTI
CASTELFIORENTINO
PETRAZZI
PIEVE DI CHIANNI
CATIGNANO
CERTALDO
GAMBASSI
LUIANO
SANT'ANDREA A GAVIGNALLA
BADIA A ELMI
MONTECARULLI
SANTO PIETRO
PANCOLE
MUCCHIO
VICO D'ELSA
CELLOLE
COLLEMUCIOLI
ULIGNANO
S. APPIANO
STRADA
SAN GIMIGNANO
S. LUCIA
CASAGLIA
MONTAUTO
BIBBIANO
POGGIBONSI
LA MAGIONE
COLLE DI VAL D'ELSA
CAMPIGLIA DEI FOLI
PIEVE A CONEO
STAGGIA
PARONZA
ABBAZIA DI CONEO
PIEVE A ELSA
GAGLIANO
SCARNA
NANTOLA
STROVE
ABBADIA A ISOLA
RENCINE
PIEVE A CASTELLO
MONTERIGGIONI
MONTAUTO
VOPINI
hospital
rectory
abbey
parish church
bridge
pavement
MONTELUNGO
PONTREMOLI
VILLAFRANCA
AULLA
SANTO STEFANO DI MAGRA
SARZANA
LUNI
CARRARA
MASSA
PIETRASANTA
CAMAIORE
MAR TIRRENO
LUCCA
CAPANNORI
PORCARI
ALTOPASCIO
FUCECCHIO
PONTE A ELSA
GRANAIOLO
CASTELFIORENTINO
PIEVE A CHIANNI
CERTALDO
SAN GIMIGNANO
LINARI
POGGIBONSI
GRACCIANO D'ELSA
MONTERIGGIONI
ABBADIA A ISOLA
SIENA
MONTERONI D'ARBIA
PONTE D'ARBIA
BUONCONVENTO
TORRENIERI
SAN QUIRICO D'ORCIA
LE BRICCOLE
RADICOFANI
ACQUAPENDENTE
BOLSENA
LAGO DI BOLSENA
MONTEFIASCONE
ROMA

motivations, which were repeated in the following jubilees.
The resumption of travelling, after the year 1000, also gave an answer to the needs of economic development, and particularly of trade. The markets grew larger and traffic, of man and goods, demended a wide and safe communications network, involving new economic realities, such as Florence. In many cities markets and fairs sprang up, attracting sellers and buyers under the indulgent eye of the authorities, able to obtain new revenues thank to the "transaction tax" that must be paid to the local authority in exchange of the permission to hold a stall. At the same time, a whole system of infrastructures was set up, to make the journey easier for pilgrims and merchants. The first to build "spedali", that is to say shelters for the travelllers, were the *pievi,* parish churches, ecclesiastical structures on a territorial basis. The most famous hospital was the Santa Maria della Scala in Siena, with a central structure and a network of smaller "spedali" along the main routes. In the territory of the Comune of Monteriggioni, there used to be a "spedale" at Strove, run by the monks of Abbadia a Isola, and one at Castiglion Ghinibaldi, besides other structures near Staggia, that is to say near the border between Florence and Siena.

105

Later on, in the course of the XII century, alongside with free religious hospitality, private shelters that gave hospitality against payment. In the cities hotels were born, while in the countryside one could spend the night in more modest inns; taverns offered to the travellers also wine and fruit. This kind of hospitality was not always safe, and wayfarers must beware: landlords were considered treacherous characters whose main occupation was swindling and robbing their clients. On this subject, there are many historical and literary references.
The presence in Siena of a Guild of hotel-keepers in the second half of the XIII century, and the control of the Comune itself over it, aimed to give a more reassuring dimension and image to paid hospitality; it also proves that, at that time, private hospitality was a well developed activity. Thus, the journey lost the features of an adventure, and became a more and more habitual practice.
Besides the maintenance of roads and bridges, allowing the crossing of rivers, the Comune of Siena ensured the presence of water springs and fountains along the main roads. Various enterprises aimed to get up to the surface, from its underground river-bed, a spring at Fonte Becci, important crossroads, from which the via Francigena and the via Fiorentina (actual Chiantigiana) departed.
Besides the creation of a fountain, it was necessary to guarantee its future maintenance, making sure that it was not used to wash linen.
Sometimes, the fountains were built in order to prevent animals

from drinking from them. When a fountain was built in the *contrada* of Monteriggioni, the orders were to "*... build a vault in the upper part, in such a way that animals will not be able to drink in the aforementioned fountain...*"
The general situation of prosperity brought on improveents in the road network. New roads were developed, some traits of the old ones, such as the Francigena, were changed. The new political realities, born in that period in central and northern Italy, the Comuni, had to take care more and more of the creation of new roads, of their maintenance and safety.
However, all this was a later consequence. Limiting our survey to the Monteriggioni area, and the via Francigena which crossed it, and trying to reconstruct the road situation from the very beginning, we have, as first evide,ce, the narrations of some religios characters who crossed Tuscany to reach Rome. The archbishop of Canterbury, Sigeric, described his journey from Great Britain to Rome at the end of the X century, also indicating the various stops and providing us with precious information on the "stations" of that time.
Particularly for the trait north of Siena, all the places touched on the route are mentioned: XV Seocine (Siena), XVI (Burgenove), XVII Aelse (Pieve a Elsa - Gracciano), XVII (San Martino ai Foci), XIX Sce Gemiane (San Gimignano), XX Sce Maria Glan (Santa Maria a Chianni), XXI Sce Petre Currant (San Pietro a Coiano), XXII Sce Dionisi (San Genesio), XXIII Arne Blanc (Arno). This evidence furnishes us with a rather accurate reconstruction not only of Sigeric's journey, but also of the general route of the Via Francigena in the northern part of the province of Siena.
In the XII century the route south of the river Arno changed, and, from the ridges of the hills, the road passed through the

valley bottom, following two different routes on both sides of the river Elsa. The first, the one on the left, is probably the older of the two, being already mentioned in the middle of the XII century, in the narration of an abbot from Iceland, Nikulas of Munkathvera, who went on a pilgrimage to Rome at that time.
Therefore, we know that after crossing the Arno, the route reached San Genesio; from here, the road left the previous route, otuching Ulignano and Torri, wading the stream Foci and then the Staggai, to reach Borgo Marturi, the old Poggibonsi. From Borgo Marturi the road passed through the castle of Staggia, and then Castiglion Ghinibladi, to join the previous route at the foot of the Monte Maggio.

Notes about innkeepers

"Some of them drove their guest out of thir inn to welcome new richer-looking ones. Some made their guests taste a good wine and then served a bad one, or directly must. Some used fixed measures. The last glass was always the better, because some of them used to rob their guests while they were asleep. Some used to poison their guests to inherit their goods, others sold to pilgrims rotten meat or fish to intoxicate them. They used to offer the first meal for free but sold candles at high prices. As a matter of fact everyone among them required high fees for wine, wheat or candles thus trying to deceive even paying customers".

The other route, a few decades earlier, was described by Philip Augustus king of France in his journey back from the III Crusade (1191).The king of France came from Rome, thus indicating the stages on his journey from south to north. Orientation will in this case also be inverted to give all the routes the same southbound reading.
From the river Arno, the route passed through San Genesio, and from here it steeredon the other side of the Elsa river. It touched Certaldo and Castelfiorentino arriving at Borgo Marturi (Poggibonsi). From Poggibonsi it went up the river Staggia on the right, arriving at the Rencine Castle and then to the Badesse plain, from which it went up Corpo Santo until Uopini, and then to Fontebecci and Siena. The Corpo Santo (Holy Body) was a special spot on the route. A leper hospital was built here, to shelter wayfarers victims of leprosy, who could not enter the cities nor could they get any closer than 4 kilometres to the city walls. On the other side of the city, in the trait of the Francigena between Siena and Rome, there was another leperhospital, Sal Lazzaro a Terzole. In the same place public hangings were held, especially of those criminals who had robbed and killed wayfarers on the via Francigena. That stretch was particularly dangerous, nont only becuase of the wading of the river Staggia, but also for the proximity of a thick forest, in which crooks often found shelter.
Communal authorities went as far as clearing the woods near the road: in 1290 the forest of Lappeto, in the area of today's Comune of Monteriggioni, was razed to the ground for 200 "braccia" (arms) on both sides of the road. As a countermeasure against criminals, the Comune of Siena on one hand gave more responsibilities to rural communities, held responsible for the safety of the route in their territory, and on the other hand gave fierce punishments to the criminals, who were made pris-

oners and hanged, and whose body was left hanging for a long time as a warning to rest of the bandits, as was the case at Corpo Santo.
The continuous development of the road network made the task of managing and maintaining it more and more complicated, also imposing frequent changes to the route, as we have seen along the via Francigena.
This must not be seen as surprising: what we are facing is not just one road, but a plurality of routes changing according to the seasons, the possibility of floods and the political situation. The border between Siena and Florence, from the XII to well into the XIII century, was a "hot" one, thus influencing the choice of the route the travellers would make.

Appendix

Monteriggioni
the nature

Monteriggioni
the archeology

Monteriggioni
the history

Monteriggioni the nature

Introduction

Soil and subsoil

Cavernous limestone: the raw material of the nature and culture of Monteriggioni. The northern section of the Montagnola appears in fact to be formed by this type of stone, of a dark grey colour, used in both **the walls of the town** (30) and the paved stretches of the Via Francigena. Limestone is, above all, the stone chosen by the creativity of Karst phenomena to model specific types of landscape, both on the ground surface and underground. On the Montagnola, one of the biggest Karst areas in Tuscany, the surface phenompena are first of all easy to detect in the two large manifestations of Pian del Lago and Abbadia a Isola. The first is a *polje*, that is to say an enclosed depression with a flat bottom, large and elongated, periodically flooded by waters which are then swallowed up by natural basins. The *poljie* of Pian del Lago, considered for a long time as the only example in

Tuscany, developes on a north-south axis for a length of about 5 kilometres and a width of about 2 kilometres: the presence of water was once around 156 and 93 hectares, and was about three metres deep. The basin was dried up about two centuries ago, and not for natural causes. The choice was to reclaim it, starting from 1776, using an underground draining canal: the works began under the supervision of the Sienese nobleman Francesco Sergardi Bindi who, in 1777, had to retire from the enterprise having spent 37000 *scudi.* An expense committment which, according to tradition, led him to financial disaster. The Grand Duke Leopold himself took up the venture, terminating it in 1781 by extending the canal by 197 metres, and forking out another 30.000 *scudi*: the result was a manufact 2173 metres long, perfectly stone-paved and brick-vaulted, two metres wide and almost three metres high, furnished with several ventilation holes. Above the entrance, situated at 252 metres in the south-eastern end of the *polje*, a pyramid was erected with an inscription celebrating the reclaiming enterprise: the most important one in XVIII century Tuscany. The second large surface Karts phenomenum is, on the other hand, a dolina, in the Abbadia Isola plain. This phenomen is a close relative of the *polje*, although different in its shape, an almost perfect crcle, and for its origin, mostly tectonics. The Abbadia Isola depression in different and long periods was the home to a pool of water, probably dried up for natural causes in Etruscan times and then reappeared in the Roman age. The monks of the Abbadia undertook the reclaimiing with various canals for the water flow. In October 1331 Abbot Feo, together with other owners, tells that "in the flatland between the comune of Monteriggioni and that of Abbadia a Isola there's a marsh called bed of reeds, where such is the rot and the putrefaction, that the lands and the people nearby are infected, and many have died because of it in the past, and the lands near the marsh are bad and sterile because they are flooded by the marsh". The catalogue of the dolinas of Monteriggioni is completed by the two ones corresponding to the nearby small lakes of Sant'Antonio and Lago Scuro, and by the many other distributed along the sides of Monte Maggio and near the houses of Fungaia, where the most important one is locally known as Valle Tonda (Round valley). The Karst phenomenum, in fact, got deeply interlocked with country life in the course of the centuries: the

considerable humus deposit (as near Casa Giubileo) gave a better chance of successful cultivations, or it could be made an enclosure for cattle breeding. All in all, the dolinas in the Montagnola area amount to 58, some of which have a diametre of more than 500 metres.
Karst phenomena are also found underground, where are many articulated caves. Currently the Catasto Speleologico Toscano have recorded 63 of them in the Montagnola area: 24 are in the Monteriggioni territory. Mostly they develop horizontally, for a maximum length of 100 metres. The deepest ones, like narrow slits, are the Buca al Vento, near Abbadia a Isola, and the Buca del Profondo, near La Cappella: they both have more than 50 metres difference in height between the entrance and their lowest point. Slightly less deep, not far from Castel Petraia, is the Grotta del Chiostraccio, with beautiful limestone concretions and impressive colonies of bats. inside it, remains of a human skeleton and of an Ursus Spealus have been found, dating back respectively to 8000 and 14000 years ago. Burial outfits have come to the surface in the Grotta dei Salami, near Santa Colomba.
The visit to these and all the other caves are obviously onlt possible to those equipped with knowledge and speleoalogic gear.
Underground resources in the Monteriggioni territory are not limited to the conspicous heritage of Karst origin. To the galleries and natural wells, object of speleologic interest, must be added artifical underground spaces, the result of mineral mines. The Montagnola represents, as a whole, one of the historical areas for the exploitation of mineral resources in the Sienese territory. Specifically, in the Monteriggioni territory the aim was to find and process two raw materials: lignite and sulphur. in both cases, the activity did not last long, nor was it particularly conspicuous: everything took place between the late XVIII century and the early XIX century, within a short productive period. Lignite deposits were found in the second half of last century near Lornano, as well as in other areas of the Sienese territory, in soils of geologically recent formation, dating back to the late Tertiary era.
During the search for new lignite deposits, **the second mineral resource of the territory was found, near Poggio Orlando:** sulphur. "Currently" - noted Manasse in 1907 - twenty workers are carrying out the excavation". Later on, the production increased and seven years later it reached the amount of 1000 tons per year. The mine,

in spite of those expectations and the first interesting results, was closed shortly after the first world war, and was tested again atthe beginning of the second war; the disappointing response did not legitimate a new opening.

Vegetation

Almost half of the limestone soil of the Montagnola is covered by a thick mantle of trees which represents the "result" of its peculiar climatic condition: fresh and humid, also in relation with the exposition and the orographic characteristics, but with an overall mediterranean balance, with the rain season in the spring and autumn. To these natural determinining factors human action must be added, to provide a complete motivation to the presence and tipology of these forests.
Man's intervention is particularly strong here, as in the rest of the hilly areas of the peninsula, which, once freed from malaria and with climates that make them apt to be cultivated, have hosted human settlements since prehistoric times. Trees here get cut down, planted, and imported in close connection with economic strategies linked with the agricultural function of the territory: for instance, the presence of chestnut trees has been for a long time of vital importance for local nutrition. This is also confirmed by explicit evidence of environmental consciousness in laws ever since the middle ages.
Whoever would cut down "oak trees or other wild trees" was subject to strict punishments.
Mixed oak-trees groves seem to dominate the vegetation at present: inside this reality, the prevailing essence is linked to the variations of the environmental parametres, ranging from the type of soil to the exposition.
Holm-oaks (*Quercus Ilex*) prefer dry areas with a limestone subsoil, stony soils with good drainage and a south or west exposition. Its habitat is on the coast, until 500-600 metres of height.
Between 10000 and 500 years ago, when temperatures were higher, holm-oaks established themselves on a higher level, until the base of the Appennines. When a considerable thermic fall was recorded afterwards, holm-oaks gradually descended.
Numerous "exceptions" have nevertheless continued living high up adjusting to peculiar micro-environmental situations. According to tradition, holm-oaks were cut every twenty years, to be burnt or to obtain coal.

Turkey oaks (*Quercus cerris*) and chestnut trees (*Castanea sativa*) prefer deep, fresh, acid and siliceous soils. Chestnut trees are accompanied by an open, airy and very well tended undergrowth, necessary to harvest their fruits. The timber had lany destinations: casings, frames, furniture, barrels, poles for vineyards, beams, baskets. Black *carpino* (*Ostrya carpinofolia*) and ashes (*fraxinus ornus*) need deep and fresh calcareous soil: they are pioneer species able to colonize but also destined to be taken over by oak-trees, if the latter were not kept under control by periodical cutting. Other presences, although more limited, are *farnie*, poplars, maples, robinias, walnut-trees, cherry-trees, plane-trees, limes, elms, horse-chestnuts. Conifers, originally not part of local fauna, are decisively a minority; mostly, they correspond to those degraded areas which have been repopulated. They are represented by cypress-trees and Arizona cypress-trees, black and white cluster-pines, yews, fir-trees and silver fir-trees, cedars. The thick shrubs are due to the climate, as well, thriving in the autumn when an unbelievable amount of berries come out: arbutus, *lentisco, lentaggine, sanguinello, agazzino,* hawthorns, *ligustro*, and, in cooler areas, cornel-trees and hazel-trees.

Fauna

Fauna, not differently from flora, developed here in close relation with human presence and activity, which, in the course of the last five centuries, was mostly represented by sharecroppers, organized for an overall productive exploitation of the territory, and therefore structurally an enemy of animal communities, considered as competitors for space and food, or used as a food resource. With the end of the sharecropping system, this trend has seen a turn more than an interruption. The abandoning of cultivations has in fact meant a siginificant reprisal of fauna, with variations determined by the advent of new cultivations. On one hand, grey patrtidges, a species strictly connected with the presence of old-style agriculture, have diminished. Hares also seem to resent hunting, besides a number of other negative factors ranging from the dominance of monocultural cultivations to weed-killing. Many animals who used to live in the woods have moved to urban centres where it is easier to find food;

viceversa, animals once limited in number by human presence in the fields are now free to multiply and are spreading fast. There are many wild fawns, roe-deersand wild-boars: the latter, in particular, multiply without any problems for the absence of the wolf, their enemy and predator. Semi-wild is the breeding of swine and ovines, which can be met in the woods. Here, at the bottom of cut down trunks, badgers, martens, foxes, weasels and beech-martens have their dens. Besides squirrels and rats, other nocturnal birds (owls, barn-owls, tawny-owls) and day birds (such as buzzards and the several types of hawks) need the forest, to make their nest in trees cavities and to use branches as sighting positions. Some of the cavities used as nests are not natural ones, but built in tree trunks by woodpeckers (green and red ones).

Underground animals appear unconcerned by the aforementioned social and economic changes, in a habitat featuring absence of light, high humidity rate, and a constant temperature.

Animals only incidentally live in such an environment, or during certain phases in their vital cycle. Troglobes only live and reproduce there permanently. Among them is a gasteropode mollusc, *Bithiospeum virei*, which, in the Karst system of the Montagnola, lives in cold underground waters, between 6,5 and 12,58. Lastly, bats are the only vertebrates using the underground environment: as a refuge for their daily rest, and as their winter abode during hybernation.

Monteriggioni
the archeology

Remote past

Splinters of stone

Above all, red jasper, and also quartzite. These were the raw materials used by the first industry in the territory, active during the medium Paleolythic and individuated in 1968, not far from modern warehouses and the Siena-Florence Autopalio: more prescisely, as the founder Carlo Tozzi pointed out, "in the cultivated fields situated between the group of houses called Sant'Antonio and the farmhouse 'Palazzo alle Frigge', about 3 kilometres from Monteriggioni". Here, during various recognitions within an area of about m 80 x 100, 917 stone manufacts of very small dimensions were found. As a whole, the finds appear typologically homogenous, although they are not easy to place within a specific cultural contest: they

certainly date back to the Musterian period (chronologically ranging from 64000 to 36000 years ago) and, more precisely, to the La Quina-La Ferrasie type, but with modalities of execution which make them an exception in Tuscany. On a national level, the only detectable analogies can be recognized in the finds from the cave of Torre dell'Alto, in the Salento peninsula.
What oher information can we gather about these distant inhabitants of the Monteriggioni territory? First of all, the human type which can be associated with this stone-age culture is the *Homo neanderthalensis*: spread all over Europe and in Africa, with a medium height not over 164 cm, this type presented both progressive features (perfect standing up position and a cranial capacity of 1450-1625 cm3) and regressive ones, such as accentuated prognatism, evident arch above the orbit, protruding occiput. The *Homo neanderthalensis* used to live, according to seasons, in caves or in huts along rivers or on lake edges; the environment was that of the Wurm glaciation. His food resources came from game, which forced him to long hunting seasons. His capacities as a smith were not limited to the fabrication of stone instruments? He could also process animal skins and make wood objects. From the objective observation that he started to bury the dead, one could hypotize that, besides solving material problems, he also elaborated symbols of a religious nature.

Bronze axes

So far, the territory has not yelded any traces from the neolythic age, thus determining a hiatus concluded by two bronze axes, which were found in the Monte Maggio area in the XIX century, and are now preserved in the archaeologic Museum in Siena. They belong to the type called "pieve Albignola", of the *facies* of Rinaldone 2: a culture which was present between 1800 and 1660 b.C. in the tirrenic area between the rivers Arno and Volturno. During this phase, society appeared as divided into large ethnic comuunities who possessed a conciousness of their identity, articulated in population nuclea of a few dozen people. Those small clans had a patriarchal structure and were mostly sedentary. Hunting still played a relevant role in their economic survival, although integrated by agriculture and metalworking. Moreover, it seems very likely that power was in the hands of a kind of aristocracy of warriors. Finds from male tombs in other areas belonging to the same culture even make it possible to reconstruct an articulated

form of fighting: first of all, bows were used, then axes were thrown, afterwards came battling axes, and finally daggers for man to man fightings.
Physically, these people were tall and slender, with long legs and arms, dolicocefals and as such archaic in the mediterranean area, where round-headed peoples were starting to take over. To complete the picture, although with caution, further clues of these first historic phases can also be recognized in linguistics. Starting from the names of the places, which can survive in the territory for thousands of years, as happens most of all with rivers. *Arnano*, for instance, is the name of a creek flowing near Santa Colomba, the meaning of which can probably be explained within the indo-european contest; where *arna* meant the bed of a river. Like the river Arno, obviously, flowing through Florence and Pisa, but also like other Italian and European rivers. An *Arno*, in Abruzzo, is a tributary of the rio Fucino; another one starts on the Adamello, in Trentino, and flows through the Breguzzo valley; a last one flows near Busto Arsizio.

A crossroads

During the Bronze age, and probably also during the eneolythic period, the Monteriggioni area together with the high Elsa valley was an area of transit as well as settlements.
"Those who glance at a topographic map of the Sienese and Volterra regions" noted Bianchi Bandinelli - taking care in highlighting the orography above 300 metres, will see clearly that the obliged pass from the Sienese basin, which we will call Arbia, to the Volterra one of the Elsa, is between the hills of Montemaggio and the ramifications of the Chianti hills near Pieve al Poggiolo and Colli."
This area, rich in hills and river valleys, presented itself as favourable for nomadic cultures of shepherds. Even more so for the Etruscan civilization, when the river Ombrone became the main axis of penetration from the coast inwards, together with its tributaries Merse and Arbia.
Although the role of the Monteriggioni area as a real crossroads is clear enough, we cannot determine the ubication of the Etruscan settlement with equivalent clarity. The most followed hypotesis places it in **Castiglione Alto**, where a high wall could in fact date back to the Ellenistic phase of the Etruscan civilization. Other proposals suggest the Monte Maggio area. However, a settlement of considerable proportions must doubtlessly have existed. So much so,

that it must have been the most important in the high Elsa valley, as it is proved by the quantity and quality of the finds brought to the surface from the **necropolis of Casone**. The oldest find that we know of dates back to the end of the XVII century, when, near Abbadia a Isola, the so-called Tomb of the Alphabet of Colle was discovered. In 1893 the tomb of the Calisna Sepu was casually discovered, in the field called of Malacena (bad dinner), in the Casone estate. A discovery which led the owner, Giulio Terrosi, to take up a systematic search which gave extraordinary results, in both quantity and quality: more than 250 tombs, from the early Iron age to Roman times, composing as a whole an anthology of types, in an area going from the field of Malacena until Monteriggioni and, on the other side, until Abbadia a Isola. The standards of Terrosi's excavations were scientifically correct at the time, but the body of finds had to go through a series of negative events. A part of them came into the hands of the antiques dealer Mancianti and was later sold the archaeologic Museum of Berlin after complicated legal controversies. The larger part was sold and dispersed, and is now in the archaeological museums of Florence, Volterra and Colle Val d'Elsa, after having been organized as a private collection by Terrosi himself: partly hosted in his Florentine palace in via delle Ruote, partly in the farmhouse of the Casone which can now be considered as the first archaeological museum in the territory. The following finds, in the XX century, are also important: in one of the two chamber tombs discovered in 1930 an Attic amphora with black figures decoration, of relevant value, was found. Another casual discovery, also near Abbadia a Isola, was that of 1982: an unprofaned chamber tomb which marks the beginning of a phase still the object of research. Similarly in progress is the interpretation of an excavations started in 1986 in a flat opening surrounded by the forest above the farmhouse of Campassini, where no burial finds have come to light, but finds coming from a settlement which can be defined as an "Etruscan farm of the oriental period". It is not, in fact, a village, with different and complementary functions and structures, but a more limited unit, well organized and self sufficient. It was active in a period of time from the last quarter of the VIII century to the end of the VII.

58
105

Oriental and archaic period

The most archaic phase of the farm at Campassini, as opposed to the following

phase, does not seem to have a parallel in the necropolis at Casone. Burial shreds make it possible to suppose the existence of another centre, perhaps Castiglion Alto, already active during the VIII century b.C., which dominated the rest of the settlements in the val d'Elsa, especially in the course of the following century. To this first period belong pit graves, with the deposition in an ossuary of raw fabric, and also trench graves: furnished with grave-goods of little value (small vases and bronze objects for personal use).
Towards the mid VII century chamber tombs spread widely, often with peculiar architectonic interpretations, the grave-goods of which seem to indicate an economic development shown by the wide cultural contacts they are an expression of.
Probably, external influences had been absorbed, often elaborated, and also spread.
From a small chamber tomb, found in 1898, comes the famous *bucchero kyathos*, today preserved in the Museo Guarnacci in Volterra, bearing the inscription *mini muluvanice vhlakunaie venel*: "Flakunaie Venel donated me".
Etruscan Monteriggioni indeed founded its prosperity on the fertility of the fileds, but even more so, as said above, on its fortunate position in relation to varoius road networks. Intense commercial exchanges went up the Ombrone valley from the coast, reaching our centre by the Roasi creek. It was also possible, and easier, to get here passing through the un-marshy traits of the Rosia plain, along the Arnano stream, going further west of the Cannucci hill, ending up in the small flatland around Santa Colomba. From here, it was possible to continue following the lower ramification of the river Staggia. Our centre had contacts with Volterra, Castellina and also, perhaps through the val di Pesa, with the Montalbano area (that is to say, with Artimino and Comeana), and, through the Val di Greve, with Quinto and Sesto Fiorentino. Even when, during the VI century, commercial traffic decreased considerably, the Etruscan Monteriggioni probably did not suffer from the crisis which hit nearby centres.
During this phase, aristocratic chamber tombs developed, hosting depositions probably belonging to the ruling class: the shreds were sometimes imported, as is the case of Attic ceramics with black and red figures.

Classic and Ellenistic period

The utmost development of Etruscan Monteriggioni was reached during the Ellenistic age, when, towards the end of the IV century, Volterra started to be important and,

therefore, influent.
The most famous tomb from this period is that called of the Calisna Sepu, from the family after whom the burial mound was named: a rectangular chamber dug in travertine, with the entrance facing west, closed by a large stone also in travertine. It hosted as many as 105 depositions, all ossuaries, in alabaster or travertine, or ceramics and bronze. On the whole, 450 objects were found there, to be placed in a period of time spanning from the end of the IV century to the beginning of the I century b. C.

Roman imperial period.

The serious and quick crisis manifested itself as for other poles of the Etruscan civilization, in the course of the I century b. C. Even though - as Bianchi Bandinelli pointed out - the shreds seem to indicate "... a certain cohesion of the old centre, lasting through a couple of weaker and weaker generations...": the grave-goods of the tombs and the architectonic structure itslef are progressivly degrading, both in quantity and in quality. The causes are to be looked for in the decline of agriculture, ruinously involved in civil wars and in the following retaliations by Silla, who confiscated lands. Etruscan Monteriggioni, in this new panorama, is not any longer under Volterra's protection and can't be protected by the newly born Siena, which, on the other hand, will represent a problem for its excessive proximity. Furthermore, viability which had determined Monteriggioni's expansion is now reduced to a secondary role. Rome communicates with Florence and lucca, and the north as a whole, through the coastal route of the Aurelia, or thanks to the Cassia now reaching Arezzo from Chiusi. Etruscan Monteriggioni, too, not differently from other centres in the val d'Elsa, got progressively depopulated until it was reduced to a *pagus*, or rural village

Monteriggioni the history

MONS REGONIS
Mons Regonis, oppidum, situ et manu munitum, magna tormentorum vi quaßatum,
praesidio metu perculso, à Caesarianis et Aethruscis superatur

Introduction

The territory of Monteriggioni appears to the visitor as possessing physical features differing substantially from one another, and on the other hand lacking peculiarities distinguishing it from the neighbouring *comuni*. The attentive visitor will soon notice the presence, around the high ground of Monte Maggio, of small plains such as Pian del Lago and Canneto (the old toponym of the lands around Abbadia a Isola), while a series of small valleys formed by creeks and streams are characteristic of the central and eastern part of the territory. The variety of physical elements is immediately registered, but taking a better look we will soon realize how such variety is continued in the neighbouring *comuni*, without interruption. In fact, excluding the river Elsa, which marks the north-west boundary, and the ridge of Monte Maggio on the west side, the other borders are artificial, the result of historical events. Therefore, we cannot but agree with Paolo Cammarosano, who, in a brilliant book on the history of Monteriggioni which we will quote often, defines Monteriggioni a space the origin of which "is not natural, but historical". For this reason, an attempt to comprehend Monteriggioni must go through the events from the via **Francigena**, the important road linking central and northern Europe to Rome, to the foundatiuon of the abbey of Isola d'Arbia (1001), to the erection of the Castle of Monteriggioni by the Comune of Siena (1213) and its surrender to Cosimo de' Medici (1554). Lastly, its following development will be examined, with traces perhaps less evident but not less important. While the most important and specific events, linked to Monteriggioni being on the border with the Florentine territory, take place up until the XVI century, the following period is rich in great changes and modifications, although often fragmentary ones. They range from medieval castles to Renaissance villas (Santa Colomba) and XVIII century mansions (Basciano), from the reclaiming of Pian del Lago to the opening of the railway line to Empoli, with the Montarioso gallery. Nevertheless, the prensence of marked medieval features (such as the towers of Monteriggioni) tend to create a sort of deformed representation, or at least a limited one, of the historical character of this area, stopping at the Middle Ages as if there had not been anything else after this period. On the contrary, the groomed landscape, the sequence of cultivated fields and woods, the old vineyards are all signs of a long activity representing the silent continuity of this land: the sharecropping system.

154

It is a silent story, made up, in the XVII and XVIII century, of statistics, famine and pestilence, all numbers behind which, in this area as well as in the rest of the Sienese territory, the neverending labour of the voiceless masses of the peasants is hidden. In the XIX century, an interesting debate arose within the community: the general picture seems wider, or, better said, we possess a larger number of documents expressing different political trends after the Unity. One of them is the diary of the paist parish priest don Merlotti, and the writings of the socialist school teacher Veltroni Poderetti. Two citizens of Monteriggioni, seeing and living their land from opposite viewpoints, who we will propose in our account to show the richness of different voices. A richness which is also visible in the debate at the turn of the century: both the mayor, at the beginning of this century, and Communist party's sections in the middle of the century, claiming Monteriggioni's autonomy towards the Comune of Siena. The first world war has left traces of death in the population: in the inscripted stones in many hamlets we find the names of the numerous victims of an event which took place somewhere else, far away from here. Things were different during second world war. On Monte Maggio, Casa Giubileo was the scene of a tragic episode of the fight for freedom: after a fight, seventeen partisans were captured and then shot in a nearby spot. The building where the fight took place has recently been restored to honour the memory of those young people, and a Holiday Home with a workshop on the history of the territory for today's young people. The relationship between Siena and Monteriggioni has always been complex, both for the Sienese birth of the Castle, and for the mainly Sienese ownership of the lands; lastly, for the proximity of the two communities. A reflection of this pattern is the difficulty to trace down an autonomous local history, as only too often a reference to the Sienese situation becomes necessary in order to explain the events of Monteriggioni. This continuous passage between general and local history can in some points confuse the reader, especially in the first part: however, it is a methodologically necessary difficulty for the explanation of phenomena which, although generated in Siena, developed their effects in the territory of today's comune of Monteriggioni.

The Middle Ages

The first signs of a medieval renaissance. Abbadia a Isola

One of the most outstanding and oldest historical places in the territory of Monteriggioni is Abbadia a Isola, the first centre around which, after the year 1000, the activities of the area started to be organized.

58

Isola, which was given such a name (island) because it seemed to emerge like an island from the waters of the marsh formed by the stagnation of the creeks descending from Monte Maggio, was one of the tenements belonging to **Ava**, a noblewoman of Longobard origins, and to her sons, Tegrino and Berizio. Their interesting genealogical tree, handed down to us, has made it possible to get to know the history of this area from the end of the X century to the first decades of the XII. Nearby, a village was already born, called Borgo Nuovo. The element probably making the place important, and which

explains the reasons for the choice, was the presence of a route of the Francigena: the stretch reaching Siena from San Gimignano after crossing the river Elsa. Ava's family owned several lots of land and castles in this area (Staggia, Strove, Castel Petraia).
Following the trend of the time, Ava donated part of her possessions to the Benedictine monks, the caretakers of the new Abbey. The atmosphere of religious fervour of that period made such donations rather frequent, not only at the foundation of a religious building, to guarantee its maintenance with the revenues, but also afterwards, in order to make it more and more prosperous. The relationship between the founders and the Church was a political patronage. The choice of the abbot was up t them, and they had the right to be buried in the church. However, local dynamics of noble families and religious power must be placed within a wider geographical contest, that of the val d'Elsa, and within the various social and political forces which during that period - around the year 1000 - were developing and getting organized.
At the end of the XII century the disappearance of Ava's direct descendants and the fragmentation of the property following the segmentation of the various lines of relations, led to a new political situation which saw Abbadia a Isola as the new political and administrative centre of the area, thus substituting the founders' family. Nevertheless, the autonomy of the Abbey was not complete, as there was another political entity to get free from: the bishop of Volterra, whose diocesis the abbey belonged to. Thanks to the support of the **papal court**, at the beginning of the XII century, the Abbey managed to liberate from the diocesis of Volterra. Initially, the Benedictines tried to avoid falling under the influence of one of the two centres, by establishing a connection with a local noble family: the lords of Staggia. As Cammarosano points out, the relationship was completely different from that with the founder of the Abbey, the countess Ava. In this case, in fact, it was the abbey who conceded several of its possessions to the counts of Staggia, almost with the aim of creating or strenghtening a link with a local political power from which to be defended.
However, the relationship only lasted for a few years. As early as 1135 the Abbey had established an important political relationship with Siena. Towards the half of the century, there was a controversy regarding the ownership of some tenements part of the patrimony of Ava's family, a dispute which forced the monks to reconstruct Ava's genealogical succession and the bequests that she and her

70

heirs had given the monastery. During this period, any possibility of a political power over the territory - autonomus from Siena and Florence- had fallen through. It was a must to choose, and take sides with either one. At first, the counts of Staggia sided with Siena, but then knew internal disagreements. Some of them maintained the alliance with Siena, to which they had offered as a pledge the castles of Montauto and Strove; some others linked their destiny with Florence.

This is the context within which the oath of allegiance to Siena was taken in 1215 by all the family heads of Abbadia a Isola, together with the near by communities of Strove and Pieve al Castello, a formal act which ratified the end of local autonomy and tied the destiny of this area to the Republic of Siena.

The foundation of the castle of Monteriggioni

Siena could not contrast the expansion of Florence on the northern border: at the end of the XII century, they had been defeated by the Florentines several times, and had to accept the river Staggia as a boundary limit, losing the rights over Borgo Marturi (from which Poggibonsi later derived). It was necessary to come to terms with some important local realities such as Poggibonsi and its allies, the counts of Staggia, therefore it was necesary to abandon any design over the castle of Staggia. However, the area was too exposed to Florence's expansionist policy and a military defence was necessary: this need, linked to the political impossibility of taking possession of the castle of Staggia, gave birth to the decision of building a new castle in the area: the castle of Monteriggioni.

It represented an anomalous enterprise, as Siena's traditional policy usually aimed at taking possession or purchasing already existing castles. For instance, in 1215 Siena had purchased the castle of Quercegrossa from a local noble family, the lords of Cerreto, and a few years later many lots of land had been bought in the same area, to unite an economical power to the military possession of the castle, with the object of extending their control over the territory. The decision to build a castle *ex novo* will remain a comparatively isolated case also in Siena's following political trends; as such, Cammarosano quite rightly judges it as "exceptional". **A stone plaque placed beside the Porta Romea in Monteriggioni commemorates the event and its protagonists.**

The building of a castle *ex novo* created problems of new population; therefore, the republic tried to stimulate the peopling of the castle by granting some privileges such

as the *status* of citizen of Siena, and the twenty years exemption from personal tax. These decisions had a positive response. In the mid XIII century there were as many as seventy-two family heads, which meant a total population of some hundred people. From the very beginning, Monteriggioni was at the centre of wars against Florence. A first one, around the third decade, even jeopardized the existence of the not yet completed castle. In the 1232 peace, the Florentines imposed as a condition the demolition of the castle. The reprisal of the war saved the castle: **in the following peace of 1235** its destruction was not demanded. At the half of the century, a new war broke out, involving Florence, Siena, Pisa and Pistoia. In this circumstance, Monteriggioni was besieged by the Florentines, and risked being conquered due to the (failed) betrayal by German troops, who wanted to sell the castle for 50.000 gold florins. A rapid peace saved Monteriggioni from falling, out of betrayal, in the hands of the Florentines; or, better said, the event was postponed until three centuries later. Monteriggioni will fall in the hands of Siena's traditional enemies for the betrayal of its commander in 1554. The lucky escape was a warning that the Sienese took good notice of, as Repetti reports: "having the Sienese learnt from the danger, they added, between 1260 and 1270, new fortifications at Monteriggioni, which they furnished with a keep with a round wall and towers, surrounding the castle in the manner that we can today see."
With the battle of Colle (1269) and the defeat of the ghibelline coalition, Siena's policy will slowly change, also for the uprisal of new social forces which will express themselves through the government of the Nine (1287). From then on, both the network of alliances - Siena would become Florence's alley - and, as aconsequence, the centre line of Sienese expansionist trend, now directed towards the Maremma and the Val d'Orcia.
Beisde the military dimension, Monteriggioni was slowly growing in the surrounding territory thus provoking tensions with pre-existing communities, and changes in the organization of the territory. The growth of Monteriggioni soon clashed with the other developing centre, ubicated within a short distance: Abbadia a Isola. The reasons for disagreement were numerous. The lands belonging to the Abbey which the Soarzi, the noble protectors, had sold to Siena as if belonging to them, the territories situated between Abbadia a Isola and Monteriggioni, particularly the **marsh of Canneto.** For this

151

latter contentious jurisdiction, the friction was tense one, soon growing into a violent fight which saw the monks give in. Cammarosano reports: "There came the Sienese citizen Uggeri, and the castellan of the Sienese commune in Monteriggioni, and the most part of the men of the castle, all armed. They beat up the monk Piero, the lay brother Rinaldo,who represented the monastery of Isola, and the scyhemen who were there with them; and so, violently, they threw them out and expelled them..." In the following year, an agreement was reached, dividing the marsh of Canneto in two parts: one belonging to Moonteriggioni and the other to Abbadia a Isola. The religious organization of the territory was also changed by the presence of the new settlement. The church of San Giovanni a Stecchi, later destroyed, became a part of the Monteriggioni territory, and so did the church of Santa Maria a Stomennano, which was elevated to the more important rank of *pieve* from being a simple parsonage. These modifications in the ogranization of the diocesis always register, in following times, the changes of residency of inhabitants inside the territory, as well as giving evidence of a concentraion of the population in Monteriggioni, towards the end of the XIII century, at the disadvantage of nearby centres, in this case Strecchi and Stomennano.
Demographic data from 1318, indicating 117 heads of the family, also give evidence of the expanding phase of the population of Monteriggioni. Cammarosano, including also the poor families, not present in the tax lists, indicates about 150 heads of the family. Other data, coming from the *Tavole di possessione* (an attempt to a first register of real property in the city and in the countryside for tax purposes which began in 1316 and was given up in 1325) allow us to get better acquainted with the population of Monteriggioni. Inside the walls, Cammarosano reports, there were more than a hundred buildings (obviously, the count does not include the tax-free ones), and the Abbazia of Isola appears as owning just one house, with a yard in front of it. This is a sign of the decadence of that monastery which we had met as a buyer in that first act of 1124 in which Monteriggioni is mentioned. It is interesting to note how among the owners of real estate are inhabitants of Monteriggioni, ecclesiastical bodies, other inhabitants of the countryside and the citizens of Siena. People from Monteriggioni are obviously more numerous (78 owners) in relation to the Sienese (8 owners). However, if we analyze the dimensions of the properties we find out hat eight Sienese families possessed 15% of the number of

buildings; as far as economical value went, 15% ownership corresponded to 25% of the overall value of real estate in Monteriggioni. That is to say, the prperty concentrated in the hands of the Sienese citizens had a higher value. The picture as a whole does not change if we examine the properties in the countryside. In this case, we can partly know the typology of the lands. The territory is still very fragmentary: the *podere* a a compact unit, with a farmhouse and all the annexed buildings surrounded by its own farmland does not exist as yet. Private property prevails: the only case of collective property is that of Poggio Cerbaia, of the Comune of Monteriggioni. The situation in the countryside appears as more articulated than that within the city walls. The presence of owners from Monteriggioni is inferior in number to that of the Sienese; there are also a few owners from the villages. A different method of cultivating the fileds corresponded ot the different typologies of property. The lands belonging to the inhabitants of Monteriggioni were still at the time (XIII-XIV century) worked directly by the owners. On the other hand, most of the Sienese properties were run using the sharecropping system, as were about a half of the religious properties. The difference in method was not a secondary one: it involved a different fiscal treatment, which impoverished rural communities at the advantage of the city (the owner apid his tax where he had te residency), provoking constant tensions between the inhabitants and the sharecroppers, of which evidence is given in the many interventions in defence of the sharecroppers and citizens by the Comune of Siena. As early as 1296, the Sienese government saw as necessary to intervene in a situation extending beyond Monteriggioni, common all over the countryside. The hostility of rural communities n some cases went as far as preventing the city owners to work their fields. Although we have a sufficiently clear picture of the agricultural situation, we cannot say the same of handicrafts. In 1317, Monteriggioni had one barber and three shoemakers. The situation does not appear much more varied in 1342, when among the working men are one innkeeper and one shoemaker.

The XIV century

Black Death

1348 is the year of the plague Boccaccio so carefully described in the introduction to the *decameron*, regarding both its Asiatic origins and its effects. The population of the city was reduced to a half over a very short period of time, and the countryside as well suffered severely from its effects. We do not have any numbers for Monteriggioni, but for the year 1382, in which population appears as sensibly decreased, with only 65 heads of the family, almost a half of the 123 of 1342 - and all this, almost 34 years after the plague.

Political organization

In the meantime, there had been deep changes in politics in Siena, which would influence Monteriggioni directly. In 1355 the government of the Nine had fallen, after having run the city for over sixty years, also ensuring stability as regards the alliance with Florence. The following governments, sustained by unstable coalitins of variegated social extraction, including nobles, craftsman, people, took up again the traditional anti-Florentine policy. Monteriggioni, the castle on the northern border, thus acquired again its strategical importance for Siena. Indeed, as early as 1361 the bridge, the tower and the bell were restored at the expense of the Sienese government. The events of Montepulciano and Cortona marked a difficlt moment in the relations between the two cities: the Florentines kept an ambiguous attitude, hiding behind the friendly role of judges in the controversy. Maria Assunta Ceppari, in a paper on Siena in the second half of the XIV century, relates an annotation of the time showing the feelings of the Sienese towards the Florentines. "Year MCCCLXXXVIII, misser Giovanni of Monte Pulciano took away Monte Pulciano from our Comune and gave it to the Comune of Florence. May death come upon the house of the Del Pecora and upon the Florentines! (...) The Florentines took Cortona away from us. Being allied with the Florentines, they should have defended Cortona and Montepulciano for us and instead they took them both away from us. In a thousand way do they tear us apart and lead us by the nose with many lies and falsities, so many that it would take too long to count them..."

A few years later, in 1390, Siena resumed an anti-florentine poitical trend in order to obtain revenge for the wrongs suffered. Not daring to face Florence on their own, the Sienese became allied, or better said, submitted themselves to Gian Galeazzo Visconti, Lord of Milan, who aimed at taking possession of Tuscany and forming a confederation of Tuscan cities under his command against Florence. In Siena, on the other hand, there still was a political party on the Florentines' side, who did not accept the new situation. The Malavolti family, landowners, who had property also in the Monteriggioni territory, guided the fight against the

Visconti, and, with the aid of Florence, they took the castle by surprise and conquered it. However, they did not keep in their hands for long, as Monteriggioni was soon won over again by the troops of Siena and Milan. To keep the memory of the Malavolti's betrayal alive - as Petra Pertici recalls - under the infamous painting of Orlando of Donusdeo, they Sienese wrote about the head of the Tolomei family "You who look at this paintings / look at me, who for my greediness - betrayed my motherland. To get florins, I sold Siena to the false Florentines". Hate did not subside even when, with the death of Gian Galeazzo Visconti, the anti-Florentine league was dissolved. Malavolti, once back in town, was killed by Bellanti and Marzi, belonging to the rival faction.
The renovated interest in Monteriggioni in the second half of the XIV century can also be found in other actions, aiming at strenghtening this comune also on an institutional plan.
The act confirming this institutional stability is the *Statuto* of 1380, in *lingua volgare*, written down by some citizens of Monteriggioni and approved by Siena. The local drawing up of the Statuto demonstrates the presence of a ruling class of a certain political ability; the approval by Siena shows the will and the interest in a political growth of the community, although still under Siena's wing.
The Statuto, in fact, dealt with the minor jurisdictional issues which Monteriggioni was in charge of, while the most important one were still the responsibility of the dominating city, Siena. The most interesting side concerns local magistratures. A Vicar elected by Siena was at the head of the community, and his appointment lasted a year. Other magistrates, chosen within the community, coadiuvated him, in charge for six months: two consuls, one *camerlengo* and six counsellors.
The consuls' tasks essentially involved substituting the vicar when the necessity arose (an usual situation, as the inhabitants often put in complaints about the unfrequent presence of the vicar); they were also in charge of defending the weak (widows, orphans). The camerlengo administered the comune's funds.
Consuls, camerlengo and counsellors appointed other 'minor officers', among which two *viari* in charge of the maintenance of roads and bridges, a messenger and a town crier to inform the citizens of decisions that had been taken, two officers in charge of the state organization and control of the distribution of food, who also superintended the weighs used by retailers, an official

who represented Monteriggioni at the compune of Siena, and an ambassador. A second section of the Statuto concerned civil law norms. There were not many, as they referred to the Statuto of Siena. It is interesting to notice the dates of juridical holidays: from San Giovanni until the month of August, that is to say during major works in the fields (harvest-time and ploughing-season); and from Santa Croce (14 September) to San Michele (29 Semptember), grape-picking time; thus, we gather the image of a rural community developing its activities in close connection with coltural cycles. The prohibitions in the Statuo also give us an image of Monteriggioni: according to an atavic custom, people probably used a strong language and blasphemies must be frequent, if a special guard corp was instituted to punish blasphemers with a fine amounting to 40 *soldi*. The measure for the observance of religious festivities were also strict, as well as those concerning gambling, which was prohibited. A list of permitted card games gives us some names: Baldracha, Buffa, Moretto.

The XV century.

Florence remains at the centre of Sienese foreign politics in the continuous changing of alliances, like in the first years of the XV century, or wars like in 1430, when Florence tried to take possession of Lucca, that had Siena as alley. The war turned into a setback for Florence, but it underlined the Fiorentine politics' lines of action, that can be synthesized in the prayer that, according to the tradition, the Florentines used during the war of Lucca: "Ave Maria, grazia plena, auta Lucca, aremo Siena". The particular events of Monteriggioni's area are not known , except that Florence tried to obstruct the traffics on the via Francigena, a road that passes through Monteriggioni, in the northern Sienese stretch. Moreover Pisa's fall in Florence's hands in 1406 tended to reduce Tuscany in two little countries: Florence, in the north and Siena in the south.
Monteriggioni's economy was principally based on agriculture; the already quoted plague of 1348 had affected a lot this economic area because of a drastic demographic reduction that continued for a long time. The crisis is testified in 1395 by the proposals of the Savi, a Sienese political body, to deviate from Siena's statutes, giving the possibility to the peasants of "Quercegrossa, Gradina, Petroio, Coscona, Mucenni, Quetole and Badia a Isola to breed goats in the number fixed by the farm's owner". The analysis that was made by Monteriggioni's inhabitants in the middle of

the XV century about the economic and social decline of the territory shows a remarkable awareness of the situation that they ascribed to the war, to the situation of borderland and finally to the soil's sterility.
Monteriggioni's economic and social crisis is denoted by many signs.
From this point of view it seems to be symbolic the unification of the Abbey of Isola with S.Eugenio's monastery, near Siena in 1446. The abbey, from which foundation we've started our run, was in crisis from a long time; undoubtedly Monteriggioni's foundation and the development of the Francigena's eastern stretch, towards Stsggia and Poggibonsi, were important causes of this situation. The chirch remained as a simple parish with the baptismal font.
In the second half of the XV century Monteriggioni was involved in the war between Florence's Republic and a coalition formed by Siena's Republic, Naple's kingdom and by the Papacy. Taking advantage from the Pazzi's conspiracy against the Medici the coalition conquered Colle Val d'Elsa,
an old Florentine's alley. A Biccherna's tablet celebrates the victorious attack to the city. Once again Siena's northern borders were war's territories.
The area's tension didn't disminish: in 1482 some exiles took possession of Monteriggioni's castle, that was briefly returned to Siena.
The XV century's important feature is the economic and social crisis testified by many records: the repeated taxes' reductions granted by Siena to Monteriggioni's community at the end of the XIV century or the census' reduction to the Opera del Duomo.

The XVI century.

In the XVI century the economic and social crisis in the city attenuated, but it showed only a few improvements in the country.
After a short period of improvemets during the last decades of the XV century, we have a new crisis in the XVI century. An agrarian law in 1501 affected the countryside inhabitants heavily. Giuseppe Chirone supply us a precise description of the goods' alienation effects of the subjected communities: "The use of wide plots of ground, whether fit to be sown or uncultivated or wooded, guaranteed to all the members of the community and exerted with rigorously established rules, made up an important social damper, and in the meantime guaranteed to the community the incomes that were necessary not only for the taxes' payment to the Dominante, but also for certain services' accomplishment, like the boundary wall, the springs and the roadway maintenance,

the basis for the development of a normal economic activity". The effects for Monteriggioni's territory, in particular, can be noticed in the relations of the different little comuni some years after, on the occasion of a report on their economic conditions, that gives an image of general poverty. Even if it is necessary not to exaggerate the declarations' veracity, because this responses were used in Siena in order to fix the community's new fiscal burdened. Siena was passing through very difficult political years and its events directly involved the rural comuni, which history tend, during this period, to flatten on that of the main town. SO that, in order to understand Monteriggioni's events, it is necessary to examine Siena's history. After Pandolfo Petrucci's death, his heirs didn't prove themselves up to continuing his action and were briefly driven away. But by that time the problem was no more bound to the internal feud among Popolari and Nove or among Nove and Riformatori (the different factions or "monti" of Siena's political life).
The political game was between Empire and France, and the time of the little autonomous countries was dyeing out, they could survive only by exploiting the rivalries among the main powers.
The Tuscan picture of still free comuni was always more reduced: Volterra was already fallen under Florence, Pisa rebelled but had to succumb. At that time in the tuscan zone the Florentines aims were turned to Siena. The old city's protectors tended to change role and showed the desire to take possession of the protected. The alliance with Charles V became always more stifling; the spanish garrison in Siena, from a defence element of the Republic's liberty turned into a strong symbol of a foreign power. This was always clearer. In fact the Emperor required always more onerous financial tributes and moreover, against the willing of Siense political bodies, he wanted to build a fortress in San Prospero for the spanish soldiers' garrison. There was a last attempt to renew the Republic's old magnificence. Trusting in France, Siena drove away the spanish garrison. It was the war against Charles V, allied with the grand duke Cosimo dei Medici that hoped to enlarge his domain over Siena. One of the first republic's acts, waiting the arrival of the enemy's army was to fortify its castles, and among them, naturally, Monteriggioni.

The siege and the fall of Monteriggioni.

The confict between Henry II and Charles V was extended all around Europe and briefly it arrived also in Siena, a France's recent alley. In January 1533 an imperial army corps entered Val di Chiana in order to wage war on Siena. After some quick conquers like Lucignano, Sinalunga and Torrita, the army was engaged in the difficult siege of Monticchiello that fell only because of the munitions' exhaustion. In the mean time the sienese army replied with action that made the imperial army's supplying difficult. At the end of march the imperial army attacked Montalcino that resisted heroically so that the army had to withdraw in June. This firs part of the war took place particularly in the southern part of Siena and testified an indirect presence of Cosimo dei Medici. The situation of the following year was very different, Cosimo organised an army that, starting form Staggia invaded, with a quick and unexpected action, the Sienese's northern territories. A first chivalry clash took place in Badesse, but the army, under the command of Marchese di Marignano, could arrive undisturbed as far as Porta Camollia, also thanks to the hesitant attitude of cardinal d'Este — the city's Governor — who prevented a quick counteroffensive. Even though, the Sieneses' resistance prevented the carrying out of Cosimo's project, who aimed to take possession of Siena with a surprise attack. The marchese of Marignano was obliged to make a trench warfare and began to conquer some fortifications that sorrounded the city and that could be the basis for disturb actions. Among other things the castles of Chicciola and Santa Colomba fell, in the territory of Monteriggioni and after Monastero that controlled the way to Maremma. The head of the french-sienese army was Piero Strozzi a commander in service of France, who came of a noble, historic enemy of the Medici, Fiorentine family, his father was died in prison because of Cosimo's will. Francesco Strozzi led a set of military actions in Florentine Val di Chiana defeating repeatedly the imperials and devastating the Florentine territory, but the 2nd of August was defeated by Pozzo della Chiana and he was seriously hearted. Profiting of the Sienese break-up and of Francesco Strozzi's health conditions, Marignano attacked Monteriggioni the 22nd of August. The castle was defended by Giovannino Zeti and through Alessandro Sozzini's chronicles and Bortolomeo Concini's letters to the grand duke Cosimo, reported by the Cammarosano, we have a vivacious picture of that event. The imperial army's vanguards arrived nearby Monteriggioni the 21st of August and, the 26th, the Marignano and the Concini camped by Castiglion Ghinibaldi. Considering the attack's difficulty the first attempts of the imperials turned into drummings under the walls in order to affect the

besieged's mood, showing their military power and inviting the soldiers to desert. Not managing to persuade the troops to rebel Marignano sent some of his officers to negotiate with Zeti in order that he gave himself up, promising to treat him as a soldier. Zeti took some time as long as the Marignano not to dally, beginning the first war's actions. After a first strong shelling immediately the 27 and the 28 of august the wall appeared ruined in some parts, but the situation was not compromised at all. After the shelling the evening of the 28 another negotiation began, it was carried out by Concini, who " was free with words and promises". At that time the Zeti's resistance's willingness fainted, the problem was according to Concini that he wanted to save his face as soldier. It was necessary to save the appearances, to convince the soldiers and the Sienese commissary that Monteriggioni was no more defendable. The solution was found out ordering to the Zeti the inspection of the castle's wells, that were found "spoilt". Zeti negotiated the surrender asking the personal immunity for him and other six people and the acquittal from every condemns' banishment.
Monteriggioni's surrender was considered by the Florentines a very important conquer. The event's news were a very hard stroke for the Sieneses. We don't know how Monteriggioni's inhabitants reacted; a little mention is made by Concini, who first supply us some general information either on the number, a little bit more of 100 among those who lived inside the wall and those who lived outside, or on the fact that they were above all metayers of Sieneses' owners. There are very interesting, even if exaggerate mentions about the spite against the Sieneses, who oppress and ill-treated them. In particular their spite was against the vicar, the Sienese's authority on the territory who worried them with the continuous fares and in this way "ruined these harm peasants".

The Modern Age

The importance of Monteriggioni as a bordering land with Florence, the most powerful enemy of Siena's Republic, finished with the end of the Sienese freedom and its introduction in the Medicean State. From this moment on Monteriggioni Looses the characteristics of bordering castle and becomes one of the many rural communities. Its events follow the institutional changes that

the Medici sooner, and the Lorena later, imposed to Siena. Immediately after the surrender, Siena's destiny remained unstable. Before it was annexed as a feud by the Spanish king, who was the Holy Roman Empire Vicar. Nevertheless the European political situation was not already fixed and this gave the possibility of different political solutions: internal province of the Spanish kingdom or attribution as a feud to a faithful alley of Spain. As far as it regards this last case, there were many competitors.
The Carafa, sons of Pope Paul IV, were the candidates to Siena's domainand this scared Cosimo I dei Medici, who had sustained the war's expenses mainly to enlarge his dominion to the southern part of Tuscany. Finally, in July 1577, Cosimo managed to achieve his objectives by reaching a complex agreement, which registered Siena's passage as a feudto the Medici, in exchange for the renunciation of Maremma's harbours and the restitution of Piombino and Isola d'Elba. Besides Cosimo committed himself to making a military alliance with the Spanish Crown and gave up the request of restitution of any credit claimed towards Spain.
The concession of Siena as a feud formally limited Medici's power and besides, in case of lineage's extinction, Siena and its countryside would have been returned to the Spanish dynasty. The chosen solution bound Medici's political form of domain.
Charles V on surrendering had granted that the ancient institutions of the Sienese Republic (the Capitano, the Balia, the Concistoro) would have been maintained. With Chateau-Cambresis' peace treaty among France, Spain and Empire, Cosimo could definitely take possession of Siena, in fact also Montalcino and the last defenders of Sienese Republic had surrendered. "From an institutional point of view, Cosimo had to divide his dominion into two states, the old one included Florence and all the dominions annexed since 1500 and the new one included Siena and the countryside. Formally, in the new state the old institutions were maintained, but a part of the members was appointed by Cosimo. Besides new offices were created, in particular those of Governor and the General Lieutenant, who had some counsellors for specific competencies (financial, judicial, administrative). They became an essential element of the Medicean power. In the city If Cosimo had to mediate with the preexistent situation so much that he shaped in his dominion two different realities (the old state and the new state), in the countryside he created new institutions that were more similar to the Florentine situation.

The numerous Podesterie (28) and Vicariati (38), structures on which Siena's power over the countryside was based, were abolished and a mixed system of Podesterie, Vicariati, and Capitanati was organised in realtion to the specific privileges, that historically every Comune had obtained by Siena. As far as it regards Monteriggioni, this community became the centre of a civil Podesteria, and in the legal sphere it passed under the jurisprudence of Casole d'Elasa's criminal Capitanato. The lands' ownership picture will not change with Siena's order modification, the peasants will always be destitute of lands and the ownership of the métayage farms will reamain in the hands of Siena's private citizens or Sienese ecclesiastic bodies. The ownership of Monteriggioni's Hospital will remain in the hands of a family, called Del Golea. The two states that composed the Medicean Grand Ducky, recognized in 1569 by Pio V, presented a different economic structure. Florence had more developed craftsmanship and commerce, while Siena, since a long period, had retired itself into agriculture.
This structural difference caused, according to some historians, a subalternity or rather a compression of Siena's economic needs (agriculture) in favour of Florence's development (craftsmanship and commerce). Actually on the general level the protectionism adopted by the Medici, and in particular the limitation of the corns' circulation, weighed, above all, on the agricultural areas and so, on Siena's countryside. Maybe more than an economic politics' choice it was a necessity caused by the Sienese countryside situation, characterised by a serious crisis. The cultivated lands progressive reduction, the continuous exodus from the countryside, underlined by the almost yearly Balia's bunishment against those "who went to thrash outside the State" and the chronic indebtment of the agricultural communities, destitute by that time of the lands' incomes, are only sme of the elements that characterised, in a negative way, the economic and social situation of those years. The picture seems to be more negative because of recurring epidemics' presence (typhus, petechial before, cholera after) that raged during the first century of the Meadicean domination. We haven't got any set of significant data about Monteriggioni's demographic trend with regard to the period 1554-1650, the data of the other Sienese Comuni show a demographic reduction for many places, for example the near Sovicille had a contraction of 67,42%. The presence of a demographic increase by a number of places, besides limited, seems

in this situation a contradictory information in comparison with the more general demographic trend. Examining the Comuni with the population's positive trend we notice that this situation is characteristic of some big centre only, such as Buonconvento and Casole, and it could have depended, according to some historians, on the farms' abandonment and on a major concentration of residence in the rural communities.
In the archive's document we find the presence of money's distribution in order to make the dowry of the needy families up, but this was a recurrent practice, which doesn't show alone a critical situation, indeed Camarosano infers during this period fundamentally stable situation and the constant presence of the farms' themselves, in the Comune's acts testifies a certain continuity.
On the other hand if we examine Monteriggioni through the lens of the demographic trend, we have from half 1600 to half 1700, according to Repetti, the following picture:

Monteriggioni

Year	Families	Inhabitants
1640	269	1943
1745	431	3171

with an inhabitants' increase of about 51%. If we look the data at the level of the entire Sienese Province, always for the same periodo, we have always according to Repetti:

Siena

Year	Families	Inhabitants
1640	13207	93947
1745	18004	96334

with an increase of about 73%. "From these data we infer a slower demographic increase per cent in Monteriggioni then in the other parts of the "New State" of Siena. Meanwhile Monteriggioni had another administratice change, it passed in 1692 from Podesteria to Vicariato, always inside the criminal Capitanato of Casole d'Elsa. The rural Comuni Magistratures provided a Vicar of government appointment, who took the office for one year and was very criticised by Monteriggioni's inhabitants because of his short presence there, and other minor magistrates chosen among some citizens, who took the office for 6 months: Priori, Camerario, Stimatori, Sindaci. A situation very similar to that described in 1380's Statute. Nevertheless even for the citizens the office was onerous so much that many renounced. The Medici's politics to look for an alliance with the local ruling class or to create a faithful ruling class is linked to the economic problems and developes that phenomenon, which the historians called

"refeudalization" or rather "the new feudal resumption". Siena's Balia Deputies expressed themselves against this politic, which limited the commerce's' freedom further on, in 1628 they wrote to the Grand Duke asking:
"[...]please do not grant them, as continuously from many side we are incited, or if you desire to give these State's lands to some feudatory, please do it with people of this city".
It is very interesting to notice how, next to the critic for the economic politics "this state lives only with agriculture's art: with the reduction of the commerce the state could feel a serious damage, that could be felt also by S.A. and all the State" and for the new feudal investitures, there is, in subordination, the request to be acknowledged as ruling class and to be the grantees of the feudal investiture because "if the feudatories would come from the place where the feud is, they certainly would try to better the conditions of the place where they have the major incomes, because the foreigners like only that Title but think to their interests that are somewhere else".
This concepts, addressed to the official, will appear some decades after in Sallustio Bandini's writings, where the Sienese abbot proposed to substitute the Florentine executives with local officers.
Also part of Monteriggioni's territory was interested by the politic of new feudal investitures , in fact in 1667, Scorgiano, Montagutolo del Bosco, Pieve a Castello and other possessions were erected into feuds (named Contee) by the Grand Duke Ferdinando II, who granted the feud the 11 May 1667 to Giovanni del fu Firmano Bichi of Siena.
Scorgiano's feud returned to the Grand Ducal crown in 1737"The apparent limited area without feuds in Monteriggioni's territory shouldn't be undervalued, in fact as Lucia Bonelli Conenna properly writes: "All the territories without feuds but also the surrounding ones were involved, and so the whole State, because of jurisdiction's conflicts and obstacles to the development of the commerce in the different zones, that a that time rose, mainly, because of the different tariff system". It is very interesting to notice that the year of the end of Scorgiano's infeudalisation is, for a historic coincidence, also the year in which Sallustio Bandini began to write Il Discorso sopra la Maremma di Siena, the writing where he supported the commerce's freedom and so the possibility to export wheat.
But this is also the year of the death of Gian Gastone, the last Medici's Grand Duke, and Tuscany, through the European Chancellorships' complex diplomatic game passed under another dynasty: the Lorena who in 1739 entered Florence in

order to take possession of the Grand Ducat. And Pietro Leopoldo, another Lorena, will publish in 1775, after Sallustio Bandini's death, his writing. During that period Pietro Leopoldo's reformation project developed, it aimed at a general level to the unification of the two Medicean States, even if with a certain care and graduality for Siena's State. Also the countryside Comuni were involved in a set of important administrative changes. In 1774 with the reform of justice's suburban administration, Monteriggioni had no more jurisdiction's power , but it was aggregated to Sovicille's civil Podesteria and was included in Siena's justice Capitanato.

After some time, in 1777, with the communities' Reform the new Comune of Monteriggioni was born, it also included the communities of S.Colomba and Strove. The Comune was included in the Chancellorship of Terzo di Città's Masse. The changes continued after some time with the Napoleonic administration. Monteriggioni was in fact lumped together Siena's Comune territory, beginning a long history of annexation and autonomy with the main town, history that, as we will see, will last during the whole XIX century and the first decades of the XX century.

The XIX Century

In the XIX century Monteriggioni's descriptions seem to be more numerous. At the beginning a still sluggish situation will be described. A traveller of the age, A. Santi, in the first years of the century writes: "Making me now for a way, now for some fields towards Monteriggioni, without meeting anything to stop in front of. [...] It became useless after the Republic's fall, it is now a miserable place, where only countryside people live. Monteriggioni's landscape and the surrounding town offers from every side the very cavernous Calcareous Stone, through which it is possible to perceive a red soil, and this is the way the soil is as far as the tufa's banks that follow one upon the other and dominate , approaching to Siena." But besides the travellers, we have also some other documents that give us descriptions of Monteriggioni's reality in that period.

In 1823, in the project for the Tuscan land-registry office's construction a questionnaire composed by ten questions is sent to all the Gonfalonieri of the Tuscan communities in order to buld a first picture of the countryside's conditions. After the Podestà first general answer, a more detailed relation, made by an expert appointed by the Comunitativa Magistrature, followed. Monteriggioni's Podestà answered to the questionnaire some months after, the 29 July 1823 and the pictures that he makes of his territory is very interesting. As far as it regards the soil's fertility the situation which comes out from his remarks is negative: "The ground [...] is sterile so the product depends on the industry and the essences used", but also for the same farm agreement as "the owners must turn a bland eye to many abuses that occur in the farms, that is to say they have to allow the peasants to make use of many goods which the farm produces every year, and especially to make them cut the wood and sell it for themselves" (the wood belonged to the owner, the peasant couldn't cut it but only the dry twigs for himself) "the fruit's production is a little few[...] because of the peasants' abuse, they use the main part of this product for their families". As a matter of fact in the Podestà's answer, who was a noble owner, such as in those of the major part of the other Podestà, the fear of new heavy taxes seems to come out and therefore some answers' guideline attempts to describe a more negative situation than the real one.The description seems to be more interesting or rather less fictious, when the topic abandons the agrarian economy.

We know that Montagnola and Montemaggio's closeness was often (also at that time) the cause of hails, but above all we have a picture of the age's agriculture.

The main agricultural products were wine and oil and the market, where the goods were sold, were those of Siena and Poggibonsi, confirming also in this case the presence of the two attraction poles.

The land was composed half by woods and pasture and half by cultivation.

These last ones are constituted every year half by wheat and half by stubble where some broad beans are sowed. The main part of the wood is made up of acorns, and the other part of coppice... At last, as far as it regards particular impositions about the rivers, Pian del Lago and Abbadia

Isola are mentioned, both are reclaimed and need to be maintained in good conditions by their owners, in order not to turn into a swamp again.
Monteriggioni in abbot Merlotti's notebooks.
The second independence war and the following Tuscany's annexation to Italy's Kingdom created tensions between the Sienese clergy and the new Italian Kingdom. Particularly according to the Church's directives the new Government was illegitimate and none could offer any sort of collaboration. Eventhough not all the clergy was close to this hostile line, a part of the priests were favourable to the unitarian movement. In 1859, against the indications that arrived from the clerical hierarchies, these priests got some funds together among the parishioners to devolve them for weapons' purchase or celebrated Masses for the Sieneses fallen of the first Independence war (Curtatone and Montanara) or finally they wrote an appeal to Vittorio Emanuele II. In the adhesions' collection there were conflicts among the different religiouses, Giuseppe Merlotti, the priest of Poggiolo, a Monteriggioni's hamlets, who was very faithful to Siena's Archbishop, tells us a nice event of conflicts among some priests of Monteriggioni's parishes, that gives us a picture of local, provincial and regional tensions. "The 2 April 1860, as always, I went to confess in Uopini's curia, in this occasion I was instigated by the priest Carlo Sancasciani from S. Petronilla, to sign a political address to congratulate with S. E: Bettino Ricasoli for his good 11 months' administration of Tuscany. As far as I understood, after the last coffee's sip, I ran away from Uopini's priest, not greeted host, and I got on the horse; but I realised that I had left my umbrella and my overcoat in the house: so I sent the tenant to bring these objects and once she had them, the horse had good legs to make me escape from the requests of these curates, who called me in the house again through the window."
Merlotti was faithful to the directives of Siena's Archbishop and he represented an important part of the Sienese clergy, if some days after Uopini's priest was "insulted by Basciano's curate, Taddei, during a lunch in the house of Lornano's priest".
And it is curious to read the news about Monteriggioni, in the second half of the XIX

century, from the pages of Giuseppe Merlotti's notebook. It is a particular representation where the controversy against the new Italian State, bounded mainly with Sienese events , interferes with Poggiolo's events, Merlotti's parish, so far from the city's noises to "encourage meditation around the past ancient things".

29 November 1865
For the first time the Gaz was turned on during the night in Siena, but many lights turned off and some of them made a green flare. In this night the city's musical bands sang in Piazza del Campo in sign of alliance, but people will pay for this amusement, that is a product of the "Age of Enlightenment".

7 July 1866
On saturday morning, 30 June 1866, 3 perquisitions were executed together. One was by the Osservanza's frairs, the other by Mr Grottanelli and his son, two famous paolotti and the last one by S. Donato's church curate, who is very famous for his reactionary feelings. A sum of money was found by the friars, nothing was found by Mr Grottanelli and 20 napoleons were found by the curate. What an orrible crime! After the persecutions the curate was placed in the carriage and imprisoned".
But also a set of notes about Monteriggioni are due to Merlotti:

10 February 1873
In this day (Monday) in Monteriggioni's Castle Place the vacuous for the public well began to be dug up at the town council's expense. It all costed £4000 and ended in September 1873.

1877
In the afternoon of 18 June the Marquis Bonaventura Chigi of Siena moved to this parish in order to find out a nocropolis in these lands. And in fact, behind some archaeological signs, I, the undersigned Giuseppe Merlotti, parish, and he with his waiter and two workers, made for the soil's plot called S. Martino and in the superior part, nearby the border with Mr Andreini, we began to excavate the soil, where, after a stones' hip made up above all of a consistent travertine slobs, we found two human corpses already burnt over a slobs' plane. We could still notice the burnt residue and the chared bones; among thme there were a few things of no value, but above all some copper armillas with their pins that the Romans

kept on their arms to gather the garments, they were used as buckles, called "mignatte" by the archaeologists, because they are similar to those of the animals; Eventhough the objects were bronzed, they were all putrefied because of the dampness. Many big bones were found, their empty parts or their marrow were full of ground. Some earthenware's wrecks, all putrefied because of the dampness and full of ground that one day was human bodies' ash.
We found many little bronzed chiselled button of many stykes, it was very difficult to recognise them because they were oxidised. Many amber's pieces were found in the middle of the buckles, these objects were neither the dead's things nor the things thrown by the friends at the moment of the burying. The amber and other pieces were well maintained although in the dump, they were not common materials in the Sienese lands. At the beginning it was judged as an Etruscan burial ground but the above mentioned pots are known as to be typical of an ancient Roman cemetery because it was clear that they were lathe wrought and not hand made as the ones of the Etruscans, who didn't know the lathe. These objects were kept in Chigi's museum, but certainly they didn't have any real value.
We hope to find some other corpse belonging to a richer person, where it would be easier to find come gold and silver or precious stones. This is to be hoped but it is not certain. The most explored ground in that situation shows itself after the rain strewn with different bronzed fails, that, if touched, break themselves like glass.

29 March 1885
Fontebecci was restored in the second part of this year, all the frontispiece with the 3 arcades was remade with bricks, iron's allays and travertine's cyma at the expense of Mrs Anna Saracini's widow, under architect Partini's direction. The cost was about 700 Italian lire.

The XX Century

The village's teacher.

The idyllic picture of Monteriggioni, presented by Giuseppe Merlotti, the Poggiolo's curate, is

contradicted by the pages that some years after, at the beginning of 1900, are written by Amerigo Veltroni Poderetti, Monteriggioni's elementary schoolteacher, who was also interested in politics and history.
As it emerges from his Mongraphy published in March 1907, in occasion of Monteriggioni's 700 anniversary: a rare set of images made in front of the future, where the original denounce sense is faded as a source of information.
"The town hall and its bigwigs, who were for life, before 1861 were in Siena without caring for anything or anybody. And the administrated? These harms seemed to be from one side or another the dependants, or rather the slaves of the dominant oligarchy, they didn't dare to utter a word, even if they would have been butchered. About 50 years ago in Monteriggioni lived only 5 families, as now, and two or three tenants; for impact the leaves were kept by the peasants to riot in its public lanes, bordered by stains and dirt. In the place, where the grass grew, the woods to be burnt were kept. [...] And then what an education if the peasant, according to them, was born to be ignorant! What a doctor and what a medicine if the peasant is iron-tempered. [...] The masters think in this way and not differently and until we will have such directors the music will be always the same. [...] The priests who should and could have moved the right complaints acting consistently with their sermons, remained in silence in order not to disturb the plots and intrigues and the calm sleeps of the provident and ineffable masters, because for antievangelic reasons they are attached to them as the Siamese brothers. Half a century ago, the town didn't spend anything for people's education; if it happened (very rarely), because everyone wanted to die in his bed, to bring a sick person to the hospital, a "barrocciaio" (cart) named del montagnolo, was rented at the Comune's expense. This cart was dragged by an old donkey, that could hardly stand. A litter, or rather a dog's bed, was formed with straw and rags. The sick man was laid on it and exposed to the sun, the water, the wind or the cold, according to the season. After a long time, three, seven or more hours, according to the distance, the harm arrived in Siena after sufferings and

hardships, more dead than alive."

Monteriggioni's town council.

Nevertheless at the beginning of 1900 the situation was in part changed, as we can see in the Town Council's resolutions. As far as it regards the invalids' carriage, about which Veltroni Poderetti had offered a dramatic picture, the Comune had signed a convention with the "Misericordia",
that in part solved the situation. "Concerning the convention with this voluntary association for the invalids' carriage to Siena's hospital; the Council at the moment of the convention's approval in the part that concerns the Tenants' carriage, makes a vow in order to obtain a change of the peasants' rates by the Association, so that it appears fairer in the tax required for the same carriages according tot he distance".
In the meanwhile the situation was changing, there was the problem for the telephone and electrical plant of Monteriggioni's castle. The inhabitants sent in a petition. In Siena Piazza del Campo was lightened since 1865, the request doesn't seem to be unmotivated. It is very interesting to read the Town Council refusal and the motivations, that tend to propose again the ideological image of a peasant, who after the work must only rest. "A collective petition of Monteriggioni's Castle inhabitants is read at the end. In the petition the absolute lack of lightning in the internal part of the castle is claimed. The Junta deferred the petition tot he Council with the proposal to speak about it in the agenda. The Junta didn't find the petition motivated on account of the fact that the main part of the castle's inhabitants, are devoted to the fields' work and so they are used to got to sleep very early in the night, so that the cost has to be considered as an optional and it is a big uneasiness for the Balance, by the light of its limited resources".

The debate about Monteriggioni's borders and autonomy.

At the beginning of 1900 a debate about the Comune's borders developed
in Siena, the debate involved the neighbouring Comunes, above all those of the Masse ,

Monteriggioni and, in second instance Monteroni.
The problem didn't concern only Monteriggioni or Siena, but it covered all the national administration as the Comune's counsellor, Orazio Lenzi, remembers:
" Decentralisation or centralisation, this is the main problem that is discussed from many years about the Italian administrative life system. A few centres with an intensive development and enormous outskirts or a division of small autonomous and independent entities. Also in this problem as in many other ones, I believe that the truth is in the middle course, that is to say in the creation of administrative corporations that can reach all the different aims proposed by the modern society. But not such to be Nations in a Nation, not such to sacrifice important interests to follow other ones, not such to be irreconcilable with that set of varieties that we can find in our country".
It is not only an administrative engineering problem but a political one, bounded with the interests of precise social groups and their political representance, as the counsellor recognises when he adds: "In my opinion the aggregation of the suburban towns in Siena has always been a guideline of the democratic programme and I ascertain it with satisfaction".
In fact Siena's Comune attempts to enlarge its borders annexing in part or completely the surrounding territories began since the first years after Italy's Unity and are related tot he particular situation created before **in 1777 by reform of the Grand Duke Pietro Leopoldo**, from which Monteriggioni was risen. Moreover the Maremma had been separated and made administratively autonomous from the inferior Province of Siena and the reform had also created two communities, with specific measures, around Siena's walls: the Masse of the city's Terzo and the Masse of S.Martino, where it had annexed the Masse of Camollia's Terzo too, dividing the little town between the two remaining Masse. Since Middle Age the Masse showed the territory outside the city's wall. At the beginning the lands owned by the Cathedral's Chapter, then by extension, all the lands that surrounded the city for a few miles, and that many travellers celebrated for the landscape's sweetness and the cultivation's care.

The Masse had a particular juridical administration that made them in some way similar to the city, from which the main part of the territorial owners either private or from ecclesiastic bodies came, and they were really very different from the rural Comunes.
Pietro Leopoldo's intervention attempted to reduce the old Sienese oligarchy's power, trying to divide the land property's power, which was bounded to the Masse, from the city's administration in order to allow this last one to be the expression of more dynamic social and economic strengths.
The two communities turned out to be weak; without a real centre, they lacked of suitable rooms until the Restoration: only sometimes after, they had some rooms in Siena's town hall, but the management was sleepy, as we can understand from the low number of meetings and resolutions.
Their weakness involved also the other bordering towns so that after Italy's Unity there was a project of the two Comunes of the Masse and of Castelnuovo Berardenga and Monteriggioni in order to unify the secretariats and the communal services.
The project didn't go on. The situation, above all, for the two Masse's Comuni, didn't improve and, some time after (1865) in order to solve the logistic and administrative problems the two communities were unified in an unique corporation: the Comune of Siena's Masse. As regards to this situation in Siena there was an augmented liveliness bound to the development of some artisan firms, thanks to the railway's connections. This situation determined the overcoming of the middle-aged walled city for a further development in free outskirts, opened to new necessities of a modern city. This demand was early felt and taken into consideration by Siena's Comune, that tried to modify its borders for a long period and to enclose the Masse's community and the surrounding Comuni, included Monteriggioni. A first but reduced enlargement was registered in 1875, when the Provincial Council accepted the enlargement for the onkly one territory where there were Siena's Comune bodies. The problem came back at the end of 1800, when the Junta appointed a commission in order to examine a possibility for the communal territory's enlargement, which included

the Masse's lands and Monteriggioni too.
In the Town Council and in Siena's Junta, which were by majority clerical-moderate, there was a breaking that caused many clashes.
The borders' enlargement proposal, made by the commission, was not accepted and a second commission was appointed, that judged the enlargement financially negative for Siena's Comune.
Only after 1900 with the new elections the political matter arose again. The new mayor had set the enlargement of Siena's Comune with the Masse, Monteriggioni and Monteroni's annexation at the centre of his political programme. The appointed commission recognised the project's opportunity, stating in particular about Monteriggioni: "And especially for Monteriggioni, that is nothing more than a plague without a centre, without any reason of autonomy". The Town Council approved unanimously the enlargement to the Masse only and by majority Monteriggioni's one (16 favourable, 8 unfavourable).
A serious political controversy broke out. The Sienese socialists too, with the moderates and the clericals took sides against the project, judging it not useful and not respectful of the other Comuni willingness.
The answers of the interested Comuni were negative, they took side against the projects solidly. Monteroni with a resolution of 4 May 1903, Monteriggioni 24 June 1903, the Masse 1 July 1903. The answer of Monteriggioni,s mayor, Icilio Bandini, was furious. He accused Siena's Junta willingness to annex the other Comuni as a way to solve the economic difficulties and in particular the costs of Vivo d'Orcia new aqueduct.
Monteriggioni's Junta minutes show us an unanimous attitude in refusing Siena's aggregation project and it is interesting to notice the quoted motivations.
"Considering how the Comune's territory has an agricultural nature and its population is exclusively dedicated at the agrarian industry and art's exercise.
Considering how the required aggregation is not supported or justified by plausible considerations and reasons either topographic or economic and administrative..
Considering instead how the special conditions of a rural Comune differ from the

nature and the way of life of a urban one.
Considering how it could be uncivil and against the fundamental kingdom's laws to take, without any plausible reason, the juridical personality off of the Comune, which has secular life and satisfies, in the law limits,
the local needs and conditions.
Considering that the proposed aggregation could cause a serious economic and moral damage for this Comune, which should, in a brief time, pay new burdens and taxes without any advantages for the village, for this reason Deliberates.
It suggests to the Council a negative vote about the aggregation of Monteriggioni's rural Comune to the urban one of Siena."
As we can notice the accent is continuously stressed on the difference between city and countryside, as to underline the risk that the city (the urban Comune) could mislead the country. Besides this was one of the reason used by the Tuscan agrarians, who were afraid of the political contagion. We have curious reactions of some bordering Comunes, that asked to take part in the division of Monteriggioni and Monteroni's territories, in
particular Buonconvento aimed to recover Monteroni's territory northern part, that it had lost with the creation of that new Comune at the beginning of 1800, with the north-western parts of Monteriggioni. At the end of the year the Provincial Council discussed the enlargement proposal presented by Siena's Comune. The political trends were different from those of the Comune, the moderate groups linked with the lands' owner prevailed. These last ones dreaded burdens of taxes with Siena's aggregation. During the debate there were also pindaric flights.
Monteriggioni's mayor compared the enlargement's request made by Siena's Comune. To the European colonialism: "This conception makes him the same effect of Europe when it states its willingness to bring civilisation in Asia or Africa by dint of gunshots."
At the end the only one proposal of the Masse's aggregation was approved, it passed with a very little majority: 15 favourable and 14 unfavourable. The decision was not quietly accepted, there were rejected petitions and the 8 May 1904 with a

royal decree the Masse's community was annexed to Siena. As far as it regards Monteriggioni the event didn't last with the Provincial Council's vote. In 1928 the Comuni of Siena, Colle and Poggibonsi tried to divide the territory of this Comune again, but Monteriggioni's suppression request was rejected by the Home Office. Another attempt was made at the end of the 1940's by Siena's communist Federation, as Vittorio Meoni, a political leader of the time, remembers.
The officially quoted reasons were, as always, those of a superior rationalisation of the territory. We should also add more prosaic electoral calculations. Siena's Comune administrative elections showed an uncertain political picture, the Left majority was reduced: Siena's Comune enlargement to Monteriggioni, which had a remarkable Left-hand political deputation, could allow an increase of votes for the Left in the city and so more certain majorities in Siena's communal seats. The proposal had a brief life and didn't go out from the communist party's sphere, in fact the discussion in Moteriggioni's sections was so inflamed and the basis' reactions so negative that it was immediately withdrawn.

The Resistance.

The XX Century great events: the first world war, the Fascism's coming, the second world war involved and affected Monteriggioni's inhabitants in the war and dictatorship's tragicalness. But they took place somewhere else: in Carso's or Pive's trenches, in the Libyan desert sand or in the Russian steppe.
When, after the 8 September 1943, the army split up, many young boys in order to escape from the army's call up and/or to fight for freedom, in that strange mix of idealities and personal interests, peculiar of that dramatic situation, took shelter in the provincial most inaccessible places, in particular in Monticiano's zne, in Montemaggio and in the Sienese Montagnola.
Montemaggio had already a tradition as a "bush" if in the newspapers of 1800's last years it is described as a brigands' receptacle. In 1871 the Libero Sienese citizen wrote: "It is a fact that everybody knows in our countryside, except for the police, that suspicious people wonder about, for example in Montemaggio, and that they arrive now in a

form, now in another, asking something to eat or some money".
Two partisans' groups of Garibaldi's Brigade "Boscaglio" had chosen, in March 1944, as their basis the House of Giubileo's family. The farm was inhabited by a peasants' family. In their military actions they had already took two officers prisoners, one was German, the other Fascist. The 28 March they were attacked. After a hour's fire the partisans, having their munitions used up, gave themselves up, on the promise to have their life saved. They were shot in a not distant place; Porcareccia. At the voluntary murder trial and murder complicity the major responsibles were condemned to life imprisonment.
Other defendants were condemned to undergo lighter penalties. But none served completely the punishment. **The place where the tragic bloody event took place is now a holiday resort and a didactic laboratory of the territory's history.**

Bibliography

I castelli del senese: strutture fortificate dell'area senese-grossetana, Siena, 1976.

F. Arisi Rota - L. Vighi , *Le mineralizzazioni a pirite e solfuri misti della Toscana Meridionale*, Rendiconti della Società Min. Italiana, XVII, *La Toscana Meridionale*, Milan 1972.

G. Bartoloni - G.C. Cianferoni, *Lo scavo di Campassini (Monteriggioni): una fattoria etrusca di età orientalizzante*, (in publishing).

G. Becatti, *Un'antica memoria dello spedale di Castiglion Ghinibaldi*, BSPP, n.s. V (XLI), 1934.

R. Bianchi Bandinelli, *Materiali archeologici della Valdelsa e dei dintorni di Siena*, in "La Balzana", 1928, II.

D. Bizzarri, *Tentativi di bonifiche nel contado senese nei secoli XIII-XIV*, Studi di storia del diritto italiano, edited by F. Patetta and M. Chiaudano, Turin, 1937.

L. Bonelli Conenna, *Crisi economica e demografica dello Stato Senese agli inizi del XVII secolo*, in *Contadini e proprietari della Toscana Moderna*, Proceedings of the meeting in honor of Giorgio Giorgetti, I, Florence, 1979.

L. Bonelli Conenna, *Sallustio Bandini, uno sguardo sulla Maremma*, in *Storia di Siena*, II, Siena, 1995.

R. Bradbury, *Farenheit 451*, Verona, 1966.

P. Cammarosano, *Monteriggioni. Storia, Architettura, Paesaggio*, Milan, 1983.

G. Cecchini, *Di una doppia falsificazione di documenti nella lite fra il Comune di Siena e l'Abbadia all'Isola*, "Bollettino Senese di Storia Patria", n.s., III (XXXIX), 1932.

M. A. Ceppari, *La signoria di Gian Galeazzo Visconti*, in *Storia di Siena*, I, Siena, 1995.

G. Cherubini, *Signori, contadini, borghesi*, Florence, 1974.

G. Chironi, *La signoria breve di Pandolfo Petrucci*, in *Storia di Siena*, I, Siena, 1995.

F. Colao, *L'età di Pietro Leopoldo* in *Storia di Siena*, II, Siena, 1996.

V. De Dominicis, I*nquadramento fitosociologico delle leccete dei dintorni di Siena*, "Giornale Botanico Italiano", 1973.

G. De Marinis, *Topografia storica della Valdelsa in periodo etrusco*, Castelfiorentino, 1977.

G. Del Zanna, *I laghi di Sant'Antonio*, in "Bollettino della Società Geologica Italiana", XVIII, 1899.

T. Detti - C. Pazzagli, *Il patriziato senese tra continuità e declino* in *Storia di Siena*, II, Siena, 1996.

E. Giannini - A. Lazzarotto, *Studio geologico della Montagnola senese*, "Memorie della Società Geologica Italiana", 9, 1970.

R. Grifoni Cremonesi, *Revisione e studio dei materiali preistorici della Toscana*, in "Atti della Società Toscana di Scienze Naturali", Memorie, 78, 1971.

P. Guicciardini, *Strade Volterrane e Romee nella media Valdelsa*, MSVald, 1939.

A. Liberati, *Archivio della Comunità di Monteriggioni*, in "Bollettino Senese di Storia Patria", 1925.

A. Lisini, *Inventario delle pergamene del Diplomatico di Siena*, Siena, 1908.

A. Lisini, *A proposito di una recente pubblicazione su la "Sapìa dantesca"*, "Bollettino Senese di Storia Patria", XXVII, 1920.

I. Luisi., *"Sapia" nel canto XIII del Purgatorio e la battaglia di Colle*, in MSVald, VIII, 1900.